50 Things to Think About When Writing a Thesis

Moving away from a traditional 'one size fits all' approach, this thesis guide encourages readers to find their own path to submission, demonstrating that the process of writing is as unique as the individual candidate.

This book shows thesis writers how to embrace the individual nature of writing, bringing their own unique identities and skillsets to their thesis. Each idea is presented as one that has multiple solutions, depending on who the readers are and what they want to achieve. The book guides the reader on identifying their own ways of working, their own particular strengths, as well as their unique voice and how to use these as tools to navigate the process of writing and surviving the thesis. It also provides practical guidance on elements such as the literature review and methodology, considerations around language and how to deal with life after submission.

Offering a unique perspective on the process and experience of completing a thesis, this book will be an essential companion for students completing a thesis at Honors, Master's or PhD level.

Donna Starks is an Honorary Researcher in the School of Cultures, Languages and Linguistics at The University of Auckland. Her research focuses on language and identity. It considers ways that we speak and write and how we manifest our varied ways of knowing and being to the world around us.

Margaret J. Robertson is an Honorary Academic at La Trobe University in the School of Education. The focus of her research is team supervision and the development of agency within this context. Her recent research considers the importance of agency through education, life and career choices and the importance of role models.

T0373629

50 Things to Think About When Writing a Thesis

Paving Your Own Path to Submission

Donna Starks
and
Margaret J. Robertson

Illustrations by Gaelle Horsely

Routledge
Taylor & Francis Group

LONDON AND NEW YORK

Designed cover image: © Getty Images

First published 2024
by Routledge
4 Park Square, Milton Park, Abingdon, Oxon OX14 4RN

and by Routledge
605 Third Avenue, New York, NY 10158

Routledge is an imprint of the Taylor & Francis Group, an informa business

© 2024 Donna Starks and Margaret J. Robertson

The right of Donna Starks and Margaret J. Robertson to be identified as authors of this work has been asserted in accordance with sections 77 and 78 of the Copyright, Designs and Patents Act 1988.

British Library Cataloguing-in-Publication Data
A catalogue record for this book is available from the British Library

Library of Congress Cataloging-in-Publication Data
Names: Starks, Donna, author. | Robertson, Margaret J., author. | Horsely, Gaelle, illustrator.
Title: 50 things to think about when writing a thesis : paving your own path to submission / Donna Starks, Margaret J. Robertson ; illustrations by Gaelle Horsely.
Other titles: Fifty things to think about when writing a thesis
Description: New York : Routledge, 2023. | Includes bibliographical references and index.
Identifiers: LCCN 2023005287 (print) | LCCN 2023005288 (ebook) | ISBN 9781032347004 (hbk) | ISBN 9781032346991 (pbk) | ISBN 9781003323402 (ebk)
Subjects: LCSH: Dissertations, Academic--Handbooks, manuals, etc. | Dissertations, Academic--Authorship--Handbooks, manuals, etc. | Academic disputations--Handbooks, manuals, etc. | Academic writing--Handbooks, manuals, etc. | Report writing--Handbooks, manuals, etc. | Universities and colleges--Graduate work--Handbooks, manuals, etc.
Classification: LCC LB2369 .S6886 2023 (print) | LCC LB2369 (ebook) | DDC 808.06/6378--dc23/eng/20230324
LC record available at https://lccn.loc.gov/2023005287
LC ebook record available at https://lccn.loc.gov/2023005288

ISBN: 978-1-032-34700-4 (hbk)
ISBN: 978-1-032-34699-1 (pbk)
ISBN: 978-1-003-32340-2 (ebk)

DOI: 10.4324/9781003323402

Typeset in Optima
by SPi Technologies India Pvt Ltd (Straive)

Acknowledgement to Country

We start this volume by paying our respects to elders past, present and those emerging. We acknowledge the ways of being at one with the lands on which we wrote this volume, those of the Indigenous and Torres Strait Islander nations, as well as those of peoples from all lands that now reside in this country, and beyond. We start from the premise that everyone has deep wells of knowledge and different ways of expressing and recording that knowledge. This volume aspires to help research candidates to learn to work within their own ways of being and doing as they engage in research and thesis writing.

Contents

Contents

Figures

Preface

This work is built on the knowledge of many. It has been influenced by the many supervisors and graduate students we have met throughout our lives. This includes those we have worked directly with as well as those with whom we had only minor interactions. Many insights have come from Margaret Robertson's research into supervision. Her various interactions and accounts have provided funds of knowledge that have helped in the creation of this work.

Another source of our knowledge comes through the administrative work that we have engaged in over the years which has brought many of the issues raised in this volume. This includes Margaret's work as the inaugural Chair of the School of Education Graduate Research Society, her presentations to various student forums in the university setting, and her new supervision responsibilities as an early career researcher. It includes Donna Starks' work as a principal supervisor, co-supervisor and chair for various supervisory committees, her work as Graduate Research Coordinator, as Director for Higher Degrees Research, as a member of the University Appeals committee and as a thesis examiner. Some of our experiences involved thesis writers who were happy with their research; some involved thesis writers who were truly struggling.

Acknowledgements

We would like to thank our family and friends for giving us the balance in life necessary to write this volume. Without their distracting influences, we would not have had the time away from our screens to reflect and find our centre. Ongoing requests to help renovate bathrooms, tend to gardens, and keep up the family farm, amongst many other small things made life interesting and gave us the strength to take on this volume and the space to clear our heads when writing was not going as planned.

Our heartfelt thanks go out to all of those who have read and commented on various parts of this volume prior to its publication. Thanks go to Shem Macdonald, Tricia McCann, Blaan Davies and Terri Pollard who read sections of the work that we struggled with. A special thanks go to Nhan Phan and Howard Nicholas for taking the time to comment on the entire volume. Nhan's comments were particularly heartwarming as Donna supervised her doctoral thesis. Nhan's useful commentary demonstrated acute understandings about how to provide useful critical feedback which caused us to think carefully about our text. Her attention to detail would make any supervisor proud. Howard Nicholas's comments were equally welcomed, not only for their extensive commentary based on his knowledge about the supervision experience, but also for his in-depth knowledge of how both of the authors work. He has co-supervised with both authors of this book on different occasions. He knows us well. Any faults in the book are, of course, ours alone.

Donna and Margaret

Preliminaries

Overview

Chapter 1 outlines the rationale for our book and the important ways in which it differs from other guidebooks for thesis writing. The first point of difference lies in our dual focus. While most books focus on either preparing physically and emotionally for the thesis journey or writing in this genre, we consider both topics as we see them as deeply interconnected. Our second difference is in the type of advice on offer. Because everyone is different, we do not believe that there is only one 'correct' way to write a thesis. We offer a wide range of options for you to think about as you progress along your thesis journey. We achieve this through a series of fifty pointers, each of which aims to help you think about yourself and how you identify as a researcher and thesis writer.

Why this book?

Decades ago, when I wrote my master's thesis, my supervisor instructed me to write in a particular way. He also edited my work in ways that enabled clearer meanings to emerge. In the process, I felt I lost a part of me. While the words sounded good on the page, it read like anyone could have written it. That thought has stayed with me throughout my academic career. This book is an attempt to help you as a thesis writer think about your thesis journey and how you can write your thesis in ways that reflect your own varied, multiple and powerful identities.

Donna Starks

DOI: 10.4324/9781003323402-1

There are hundreds of books (and even more articles) that provide advice about thesis writing. This is because guidebooks have a range of uses, and audiences. If you are a thesis writer with little writing experience, you may find guidebooks useful because writing a thesis is different from writing an assignment. Those of you with lots of experience writing in other genres may find guidebooks useful for other reasons. For example, if you have experience writing business texts for the workplace, you may find thesis writing challenging. If you are uncertain about writing in a western English academic context, guidebooks can also have their benefits.

With advice everywhere, how do you decide which guidebooks to read? Sometimes, guidebooks are tailored to particular types of theses. You can find guidebooks that offer advice about writing doctoral dissertations (Bolker, 1998; Brause, 2015; Dunleavy, 2003; Durkin, 2021; Harrison, 2010; Kamler & Thompson, 2014), master's theses (Biggam, 2017; Glanz, 2006; Hart, 2005; Nygaard, 2017; Woodrow, 2019) and smaller thesis projects that form part of a bachelor's degree (Peters, 2017; Lipson, 2018). Sometimes guidebooks aim to be relevant to more than one type of degree (for example, Naoum, 2019; Prunckin, 2021; Simon, 2005 address doctoral and master's research). While advice in any thesis guidebook will have some relevance to all thesis writers, in many cases, the advice in the different guidebooks contains a lot of overlap.

Another difference between guidebooks relates to their discipline of study. Sometimes the advice on offer covers general fields of study, such as writing in the social and behavioural sciences (Lunenburg and Irby, 2008) or the social sciences (Burnett, 2009; Hart, 2005). Sometimes the advice is field-specific. You can find guidebooks aimed at writing for applied linguistics (Woodrow, 2019), project management (Naoum, 2019), business and management (Brown, 2006); criminal justice (Prunckin, 2021), education (Durkin, 2021; Glanz, 2006), human geography (Peters, 2017) and social work (Carey, 2009), to name but a few. The above examples are from the social sciences as this is where our book fits. If your research is based in the natural sciences, a quick library search will uncover many guidebooks for you. While some of the advice on offer will differ based on the field of study, in other instances, the provided examples may be the only real difference between guidebooks in two related disciplines.

Guidebooks also differ in the nature of advice on offer. Some offer broad advice, others advice in specific areas. For example, some guidebooks concentrate on methodological issues, such as how to write a dissertation using quantitative methods (Lunenburg & Irby, 2008). Others focus on qualitative methods (Carey, 2009; Meloy, 2002) and specific types thereof (i.e., Peoples, 2021 focuses on writing a thesis from a phenomenological approach). Still others home in on parts of the research process, from writing a research proposal (Simon, 2005) or a literature review (Efron & Ravid, 2019) to understanding your 'contribution to knowledge' (Hammond, 2022), to simply getting the job done (Naoum, 2019; Single, 2010). Others, such as Mewburn (2020), debunk myths surrounding PhD practices. Still others concern themselves with how particular types of writers can make their way through their thesis-writing endeavours, such as Paltridge and Starfield (2019) on writing a thesis when English is an additional language. It is useful to pick through guidebooks to find those that offer you the most help as you need it.

In the end, you will find one or two guidebooks that you find useful. Different books suit different writers because each of you will have your own perspectives on what is useful. When we were preparing this book, several works stood out for us because of their approach and clarity: Rowena Murray's (2011) general book on thesis writing, Lynn Nygaard's (2017) publication on how to write a master's thesis, and Barbara Kamler and Pat Thompson's (2014) work, written to help supervisors. We also found Waring and Kearins' (2022) edited volume of thesis survival stories a great read. We liked Waring and Kearins' work because it offers a range of perspectives about the thesis journey.

So why do you need yet another guidebook? What does our guidebook book have to offer?

The primary focus of our book is you and helping you understand the multiple ways that you can write yourself into your thesis. Because of our focus, we challenge a common assumption that there is 'one' correct way to write a thesis. While a 'one-size-fits-all' approach can be a very comforting thought for those embarking on a thesis, you will find that this is not the reality. As you progress along your thesis journey, you will notice that your supervisor writes in ways that are different from the guidebooks. You will also find theses in your discipline that demonstrate a range of writing styles. The fact is, we all write differently!

To begin to understand your ways of writing, we recommend that you start by reading extensively. This includes general guidebooks on thesis writing, theses written by previous students, as well as readings in your field of research. As you read, we ask you to pay attention to pieces of writing where you may not be entirely satisfied with what is on offer. If you find yourself thinking that this doesn't sound like how 'I' would like to represent 'myself' on the page, stop for a moment and observe what *is* on the page. Does the writing seem too dense/wordy, dry/flowery, impersonal/personal, or formal/ informal? Each of us has our own perspective on how to write. The different perspectives arise from different views of what it means to be an academic writer.

While there are certain common parameters to writing academic text, there are different interpretations of what this means. The problem is: what you consider to be too dense/dry/impersonal/formal will not be too dense/ dry/impersonal/formal for the next thesis writer. Writing a thesis is full of conundrums. You need to feel satisfied with your writing, but at the same time meet the required standard in your discipline (whatever that may be).

Some differences in ways of writing are time-based. Guidebooks for thesis writing in the 1950s sometimes offer very different advice than those written more recently. The use of passive sentences in early guidebooks and the use of the pronoun 'I' in more recent ones are good examples of changing trends in language use over time. Because supervisors tend to be older than the thesis writer, they may have different views of writing. This is not always the case. Some older supervisors may prefer newer writing styles.

Educational training can also influence how you write. You may have adopted particular ways of writing from a teacher or lecturer who had specific writing requirements. You may have picked up certain writing features from texts you have read. You may have even picked up ways of organizing your thoughts from your parents.

Intentionally or not, combinations of outside influences have affected your ways of writing and made them different from everyone else. You can see some differences by doing a quick comparison of an academic assignment written by you and your friends. The ways that you construct your arguments, the length of your paragraphs and sentences, the preferred ways that you structure your sentences, and your preferences for certain words can and often do differ. There are many, many other possible differences. These differences reflect your unique ways of expressing yourself. They make your text sound like you.

Yet differences in writing styles can create issues when writing a thesis. When you try to rework someone else's sentence structures so as to introduce their concepts into your text, you can find yourself feeling frustrated and confused. It is not easy to meld your ways of being and doing with words, phrases and sentences written by others. To represent yourself in your text, you need to be able to raise your voice above the various other voices of authors described in your thesis to give it a steady consistent flow.

You can expect that as you progress in your thesis journey, your voice – and how you wish to reflect it in your thesis – will grow in confidence as a researcher and thesis writer and the ways that you write will change.

What each chapter in our book offers

The book is divided into seven chapters associated with fifty different pointers aimed at helping you think about you. These pointers are divided into five categories: existing ways of knowing being and doing; emerging identities as a researcher and writer; how you want to write yourself into your thesis; how you can heal and support yourself along the way; and how to celebrate your success.

Chapter 1 began by explaining how this book is different from many others, and how this writing guide may be useful to you in your thesis journey. In Chapter 2, we introduce a series of pointers that ask you to try and tease out your varied ways of knowing, being and doing and how these might influence your thesis journey. These pointers aim to provoke you to reflect on how you wish to bring yourself into your thesis. Understanding how much (and which parts) of yourself you want to write into your thesis plays an important part in what and how you write.

Chapter 3 takes as its focus your emerging identities as a researcher, supervisee and thesis writer, new and imagined identities that you may not have explored before embarking on your thesis. Here, we consider questions about what kind of researcher, supervisee and thesis writer you want to be. In this chapter, to help you along, we ask you to begin to reflect on how your researcher and thesis writer identities are different from other thesis writers.

Chapter 4 challenges you to consider how the various chapters of your thesis might fit together. In this chapter, we ask you to think about the various ways that you are embedded into the major parts of your thesis. Our aim in this chapter is to prompt you to think about how you might want to express yourself in the various parts of your thesis (perhaps in different ways in different chapters), while still maintaining a coherent and confident voice that reflects you.

Chapter 5 moves from the overall design of your thesis to the detail of how small changes to your writing affects how you present yourself in your thesis. Each choice (whether conscious or not) affects your readers' perceptions of your work, and even their perceptions of you as an academic. Are you choosing writing resources that give you the impact you envisage? In this chapter, as throughout the book, we take the perspective that there is no single way of writing.

Chapter 6 shifts away from writing to the impact that the thesis journey might have on you. This sort of information is frequently missing from thesis writing guidebooks, and yet it is a chapter that begs to be included. The aim of this chapter is to forewarn you about common problems and forearm you with potential ways forward so that you complete your thesis. We have yet to meet anyone who has written a thesis without one type of drama or another. Sometimes the dramas are personal ones that occur to you or your nearest and dearest. Sometimes they are academic in nature. Your research may hit unexpected obstacles or supervision issues may hamper your progress and affect your timelines. There are ways of meeting these challenges and you will find a way through them. For a small minority, your thesis journey may involve you deciding that other things in life are more important.

Chapter 7 focuses on the end of your journey. The information contained in this chapter is often omitted from guidebooks, as if you somehow vanish into the unknown when your task is done. You need closure and, with it, new identities. How do you reposition yourself as a new graduate? How do you become that future self you envisaged? Submitting a thesis is often compared to giving birth, the agony and ecstasy of the moment when you finally release your magnus opus. And then comes the void of postpartum, the terrible waiting for your examination results. What can you do with this time? This chapter provides some suggestions as well as some notes about publishing your thesis and traps that lie in wait for the unwary.

How to use this book

This book aims to help you question the various ways in which you might embed your personal, researcher and thesis writer identities in your thesis. It is intended for thesis writers, although supervisors may find its contents useful in advising their students.

The book is written with the tired reader in mind. Each pointer is relatively short with minimal academic references. The included references are for those who feel that they need more information in specific areas.

This book aims to provide you with a skillset that will help you to understand writing differences and write in ways that are more than satisfying for you. The book is organized to correspond to the thesis journey. You can read it from start to finish for insights into how you might embark on your journey. Alternatively, you might browse through the book, noting what each chapter sets out to do and focus on the chapters that best correspond to your current stage in your thesis. Alternatively, you can keep the book on hand and dip into specific pointers as you feel the need. As thesis writing is a transformative process, you may revisit some pointers in your thesis journey. You may even find that you want very different answers to how you wish to represent your researcher and thesis writer identities at different stages of your journey.

Our hope is that this book encourages you to take care of yourself and to embrace who you are and who you want to be as you progress through your thesis journey. The book is intended to help you make changes of importance to you. Changes concern both how you work and how you write your thesis. Even small changes to how you work have the potential to make big differences to how you feel. Small differences in your writing, as Canagarajah (2022) recently wrote, have the power to make big differences to your identity as a researcher and thesis writer. Perhaps some of your small changes might influence the ways future thesis writers write their theses.

We hope this you enjoy the book as much as we enjoyed writing it.

References

Bolker, Joan. (1998). *Writing your dissertation in fifteen minutes a day: A guide to starting, revising, and finishing your doctoral thesis*. Holt.

Brause, Rita S. (2015). *Writing your doctoral dissertation: Invisible rules for success*. Routledge.

Brown, Reva Berman. (2006). *Doing your dissertation in business and management: The reality of researching and writing*. Sage.

Burnett, Judith. (2009). *Doing your social science dissertation*. Sage.

Canagarajah, Suresh. (2022). Language diversity in academic writing: Toward decolonizing scholarly publishing. *Journal of Multicultural Discourses, 17* (2), 107–128. https://doi.org/10.1080/17447143.2022.2063873

Carey, Malcolm. (2009). *The social work dissertation: Using small-scale qualitative methodology*. Open University Press.

Dunleavy, Patrick. (2003). *Authoring a PhD: How to plan, draft, write and finish a doctoral thesis or dissertation*. Bloomsbury.

Durkin, Diane Bennett. (2021). *Writing strategies for the education dissertation*. Routledge.

Efron, Sara Efrat, & Ravid, Ruth. (2019). *Writing the literature review: A practical guide*. The Guilford Press.

Glanz, Jeffrey. (2006). *Fundamentals of educational research: A guide to completing a master's thesis*. Christopher-Gordon.

Hammond, Michael. (2022). *Postgraduate thesis and dissertation writing for success*. Routledge.

Harrison, Steven. (2010). *How to write a PhD in less than 3 years: A practical guide*. AuthorHouse.

Hart, Chris. (2005). *Doing a masters dissertation*. Sage.

Kamler, Barbara, & Thompson, Pat. (2014). *Helping doctoral students write: Pedagogies for supervision*. (2nd ed.). Routledge.

Lipson, Charles. (2018). *How to write a BA thesis: A practical guide from your first ideas to your finished paper*. The University of Chicago Press.

Lunenburg, Fred C., & Irby, Beverly J. (2008*). Writing a successful thesis or dissertation: Tips and strategies for students in the social and behavioral sciences*. Corwin Press.

Meloy, Judith. (2002). *Writing the qualitative dissertation: understanding by doing*. Lawrence Erlbaum.

Mewburn, Inger. (2020). *How to tame your PhD thesis*. (2nd ed.). Whisperer Books. https://thesiswhisperer.com.

Murray, Rowena. (2011). *How to write a thesis*. (3rd ed.). Open University Press.

Naoum, Shamil G. (2019) *Dissertation research and writing for built environment students*. (4th ed). Routledge.

Nygaard, Lynn P. (2017). *Writing your master's thesis: From A to Zen*. Sage.

Paltridge, Brian, & Starfield, Sue. (2019). *Thesis and dissertation writing in a second language: A handbook for students and their supervisors*. (2nd ed.). Routledge.

Peoples, Katarzyna. (2021). *How to write a phenomenological dissertation: A step-by-step guide*. Sage.

Peters, Kimberley. (2017). *Your human geography dissertation/designing, doing, delivering*. Sage.

Prunckin, Hank (2021). *Writing a criminal justice thesis*. Bibliologica Press.

Simon Marilyn, K. (2005). *Dissertation and scholarly research: Recipes for success; A practical guide to start and complete your dissertation, thesis, or formal research project*. Kendall/Hunt.

Single, Peg Boyle. (2010). *Demystifying dissertation writing: A streamlined process from choice of topic to final text*. Stylus.

Waring, Marilyn, & Kearins, Kate. (2022). *Practical advice on getting through your PhD or masters thesis*. Bridget Williams.

Woodrow, Lindy. (2019). *Doing a master's dissertation in TESOL and Applied linguistics*. Routledge.

Understanding yourself and preparing yourself for the journey ahead

Overview

At one time in my life, I was a potter. I was a very good potter after I learned that the only way to centre the clay on the wheel was to first centre myself. Once the clay was centred, I could then shape the vessel with confidence. Being centred allowed me to play with various shapes and forms. I could create utility items like sets of mugs or, with a flourish, create a unique piece of art. The same centring principle applies at each step of production, through turning and decorating.

Locating your centre brings focus, confidence, and self-expression to your work.

Margaret Robertson

This chapter is about reflecting on your ways of knowing, being and doing so that you can centre yourself in your thesis journey. This involves under-standing who you are and how you like to work so that you can choose whether to bring yourself into your writing a lot or a little, and how. If you know who are and how you work best, you are better positioned to perform the researcher and thesis writer identities you want.

In this chapter we introduce a set of four pointers for you to consider for paving your path to a successful thesis. The pointers are centred around top-ics that concern all thesis writers. These pointers focus on understanding yourself, staying healthy, nurturing personal relationships and developing academic support networks to help on your path to a successful thesis. These four pointers are about understanding who you are and who can help you in your thesis journey. The pointers set the stage for Chapter 3 and your emerging identities as a researcher and thesis writer.

DOI: 10.4324/9781003323402-2

Figure 2.1   You as a thesis writer

1. Understanding yourself: A pathway to success

You have different ways of knowing, being and doing, including ways of communicating, that influence how you think and see the world. Some of your ways stem from intrinsic capacities. Others have been learned early in life or have emerged and strengthened through your life journey. Your intrinsic capacities, coupled with your life experiences from home, school, community, workplaces and social contexts, have helped to create a unique 'you' and have affected how you see the world, how you see yourself and how you work within it.

Your existing ways of knowing, being, doing and communicating are reflected in your research in multiple ways. They emerge through the choices you make about who you research, what you research, the theoretical and methodological framings you choose for your research, the ways that you interpret your data, how you work on your thesis, and even the words that you use to construct your text.

Understanding your ways of knowing

We begin with ways of knowing. Not everyone sees the world in the same way (Browne & Nash, 2010), or experiences it in the same way. Your experiences and your ways of knowing are reflexive with each shaping the other, changing how you engage with, and the ways that you see, your experiences in your world.

Your ways of knowing offer you ways of exploring the world and explaining phenomena in your thesis. Each can play an important role in how you conduct your research and interpret your data. Think for a moment about your knowledge systems. How might you use them to inform your thesis? If you come from a society with a non-Western knowledge system, don't dismiss your ways of knowing because the literature that you are reading is centred in a Western knowledge system. Indigenous and Eastern knowledge systems are increasingly being used to explore and elaborate on how local and contextual understandings bring together understandings of different physical and spiritual worlds. Most supervisors are interested in knowledge-building, and curious about alternative ways of knowing that help to create and interpret knowledge in new ways. In your thesis journey, let your supervisor(s) into your world. Speak up about your ways of interpreting the world relevant to the topic at hand. Your ways of understanding may help to build connections and deepen understanding.

Your ways of knowing may even help you to contest ways of knowing that others assume to be true. For example, Wohling (2009), an ethnoecologist working in Northern Australia, used his knowledge of Indigenous ways of knowing to challenge Western ways of knowing. His work explains that it is not always possible to generalize knowledge about geological formation, flora and fauna of a specific place to other places.

Your ways of knowing have other uses. They can be beneficial for constructing your research design. If you come from a culture that has strong traditions of oral learning, with knowledge taught through songs, stories and dance, your ways of knowing have the potential to open up exciting ways of collecting your data. Sometimes you can even use ways of knowing to structure the entire thesis. A cultural or religious metaphor can be very useful in bringing an idea to life or explaining the reasons why or how your data was collected as it was. Ways of knowing can also be powerful for defining your key terms. Many of you may speak or read a language other than English. Words in languages often have similar, but slightly different meanings. A word from another language might help explain why a word in the English academic literature is less than ideal.

In some instances, your ways of knowing might cause internal struggles within yourself. You may find yourself engaging with multiple ways of knowing because different ways of being form an integral part of who you are. Kirsten Smiler (2016) provides a useful example of this. She reports on her PhD research, the struggles she faced trying to work within a Western knowledge system, and how she ultimately drew on her multiple ways of knowing as a Māori from a Deaf family to make her thesis work for her. We all have different knowledge systems. Spend some time thinking about how you connect with each of them. Which parts of your many ways of knowing would you prefer to use in your thesis? You can draw on more than one.

Some of your existing ways of knowing may run counter to ways of knowing as a researcher. One requirement of research is that knowledge is examined critically. Articulating your ways of knowing can help your reader to understand your positioning within the text (even if they don't agree with your perspective). You might want to consider questions such as the following: Do you hold beliefs that might make you assume your participants think in a certain way? Are you asking questions to your participants that gather data from only one side of issue (or mostly from one side)? Be upfront with your thinking and engage in dialogue about potential biases in your supervisory team before your examiners raise the issues in their examination reports.

For further reading on ways of knowing, Nguyet Nguyen and Robertson (2022) explore how Vietnamese thesis writers develop more confident and autonomous identities by finding cultural ways to shape and empower themselves as researchers. Singh, Manathunga, Bunda and Qi (2016) demonstrate the power of bringing together different perspectives to enhance understandings and show how these intersections open opportunities for thinking and writing differently. Smiler (2016) is also a good read.

Understanding your ways of being and doing

Another important way to prepare for your thesis journey is to consider your ways of being and doing. We consider these together in one section because who you are and what you do are deeply interconnected.

Your ways of being and doing affect how much of yourself you divulge in your thesis. How much (of who you are) are you comfortable sharing in your thesis? You do not need to be front and centre in your thesis if you don't want to be. There are aspects of yourself that you may choose not to reveal for personal, cultural or religious reasons.

When you think about who you are, you may want to think about what you do well. You may be great at organizing, you may also have brilliant time management, you may think succinctly or deeply, you may be very practical. You may read carefully for detail, or you may be really good at searching for relevant research articles, dealing with supervisor comments, or writing, editing or proofreading. You may be adept at giving seminars.[1] You may deal confidently with university protocols. There will be tasks in which you excel. Keep track of your strengths and how you can use them to bring your thesis to a successful completion. Take time to celebrate what you can do with ease.

We all like to organize our lives in different ways. For some of you, you may see your personal and research life as deeply interconnected. You may want to write at home or work on the kitchen table while your family surround you. You may revel in the idea of engaging your children as participants in your study, even though this may create turmoil. Some of you may like to keep your personal and researcher lives separate. You may not wish to bring your children anywhere near the university nor use examples from your personal life when composing your thesis. Each way of being and doing has its own challenges. You may have firm ideas about keeping your family close. Yet as you go along your thesis journey, you will relish time alone to focus. If you have firm ideas about separating research and family, there will be times when you will find it to be impossible to separate them entirely. Family and friends need to be driven places in the middle of the day and they require your help when they fall sick or have special celebrations. You can't sneak out to download an article while your children are jumping on bouncy castles, or your mother is blowing out birthday candles – even though there are times in your thesis journey when you might like very much to do so.

Your thesis will also involve changes to your existing ways of being and doing. You will need to think about yourself in different ways. Others around you may be very proud of your academic achievements, but they may have little understanding of why you are so busy with your thesis when you don't have scheduled classes or assignments. You may find it difficult explain to them why your thesis takes up so much of your time and attention, and this can be stressful. You may want to reflect on how you can best work in other commitments. If you have extensive commitments (religious or cultural, or social), you need to schedule times to work your thesis around your life. For others of you, community involvement may be needs-based, and you may not know when you will be called upon. What events do you need to attend? How often? How can you organize yourself so that you are not just 'being there', but also present in mind and spirit?

Consider how you can organize your life so that you can maintain progress with your thesis. What are you willing to forego? If don't plan for changes to your ways of doing, you can become anxious and unsettled throughout your thesis journey. It is best to get discussions started with those around you before you engage in your thesis. Initial talks won't solve all issues that emerge, but they will open avenues for discussion. You may have times when you need to take breaks or holidays to accommodate your religious, cultural or family observances.

How you interact with your supervisor(s) and those who occupy your shared workspace at university may need some consideration as well. Some of your cultural or religious identities and their associated ways of being and doing may not always be fully understood by supervisors, or those who occupy your shared workspace. To engage comfortably in catered social events, such as conferences, you may need to request special dietary items, or to be seated at tables that do not have alcohol. There may also be times when you are fasting when you need to reconsider your workload or writing tasks. In some religious cultures, unmarried males and females have limits on their interactions. This might affect your willingness to attend group supervision sessions or restrict who can be present in your shared office space. If you are female and wear a face covering, you may feel like you want to remove it in the presence of a female supervisor. If you are open about such things and what is required, it can happen. If you have particular needs, it is best to communicate these to your supervisor(s) early in your thesis journey. Communication is vital.

Finally, your thesis is a public document. If you are not already open about your gender or sexual orientation or aspects of your cultural or religious background, and you mention these in your thesis, you may need to prepare yourself for public exposure.[2]

Understanding your ways of communicating

Your ways of communicating are deeply engrained in your ways of being and doing. We all communicate in different ways, some of which are helpful for your thesis journey, others not so much.

If you have grown up in a context where you expect elders to speak and you to listen, you are probably an excellent listener. This is good but you may need to develop greater confidence for speaking up in supervision sessions, especially when your ideas differ from those of your supervisor(s). In this context, speaking up can be challenging. You may need a certain amount of relearning and practice before you feel centred enough to speak up with confidence. Give it time and you will get there.

For others of you, listening may not be your forté. You may have to centre your listening skills. Being an effective listener (with your ears, eyes and heart) will prove important in developing a strong researcher identity. Are you someone who listens carefully to feedback from supervisors and those with whom you share your work, especially when you don't agree with what they are suggesting (see Pointer 7 for information about supervision). You can't learn from others if you don't truly listen to what they have to say. Good listening skills have many benefits. They assist you greatly when you present work at conferences or at seminars when you respond to questions. If listening attentively is a 'work in progress', you can get good at it if you practice.

In some cases, you and your supervisor(s) might differ in the ways that you communicate. There is one type of difference that can be potentially quite unnerving. In your supervision sessions, and in email correspondence, how do you address your supervisor(s)? Do you use address your supervisor(s) as Dr X, or sir/ma'am, by their given name, or in some other way? If your supervisor asks you to address them by their given name, and you are uncomfortable with this, you can ask if you can address them differently. If they ask how you would like to address them, be honest. It will make you more comfortable in your supervision sessions.

There may be additional differences between you and your supervisor(s) that can affect your communication. In your supervision team or study group, you might want to consider whether you position yourself approximately in the same position as everyone else, nearer to the person next to you, or further away? If you position yourself closer or further away from where the person you are talking to expects you to sit or stand, you can send messages of being too intimate, or too distant, standoffish, or even disinterested. If you or your supervisor(s) are shifting slowly away from one another, it may mean that one of you is too close and the other is feeling uncomfortable. Similarly, differences in eye contact and hand gestures can unsettle communication. It may be difficult to do anything about these differences. If you are aware that it could be your non-verbal cues that may be affecting your interactions rather than the content of what you just said, you may be less disturbed about it.

Another form of communication in your thesis journey is writing. Writing a thesis is challenging, no matter who you are. Sometimes the challenges can be unexpected. You may have excellent English language abilities, but you may find that you are still not prepared. The English language you have been taught or learned may not fit with your thesis writing. Some of this may be to do with content. You may find that you don't back up your ideas with enough examples or evidence, or that you give too much detail.

Some existing ways of writing can be useful. If your writing is forthright and assertive in tone, you might find this is helpful for traditional thesis writing styles. This style of writing is useful for bringing thoughts together. For some of you, you bring passion into your writing. Some passion is good in thesis writing. It keeps your reader from falling asleep. Writing in ways that show you are truly interested in your topic can make your readers excited about your topic.[3]

Another consideration is the language you use when you write. You may have been taught English with a heavy emphasis on writing styles that are distanced and impersonal. For example, you may have been taught to use passive sentences and write in overly formal ways. You may not have been taught how to bring yourself into your thesis writing. Or your English language learning may have focused on spoken English, and your written English may be too informal. You may feel as if you need to learn English all over again. While some aspects of your English may require some adjustment, remind yourself that you know how to write in English. You just may need to tweak some of the ways that you write.

If you have been writing in particular genres for years you may have to learn new ways of writing, as thesis writing is a different sort of writing than many other types of research-based texts (Morley, 2005). Chapters 3–5 focus in on the multiple ways that you can craft your text to reflect who you want to be as a researcher and thesis writer.

As a final point, communicating about your thesis is not always just between you and your supervisor(s), or fellow researchers. How you communicate with your family and friends and community about your thesis is important. Talking about your research with family and friends can potentially bore them to death, if they don't understand the concepts or the words that are used. Even worse, they may think that you are becoming conceited if you introduce several multi-syllabic words that they have never heard before. If you know how to communicate about your thesis in simple straightforward language, others can take your thesis journey with you. If you normally (or even occasionally) speak a language other than English at home or in social contexts with friends, you could try to communicate your ideas in that language. Speaking in your other language could help you clarify your thoughts. It might also help to bring your family along your thesis journey with you, one of many potentially useful steps to maintaining your emotional health.

For further insights into one way of communicating, terms of address in university settings, we recommend Formentelli and Hajek (2016).

2. Staying healthy

While understanding who you are and how you work is important, it is equally important to stay healthy. Maintaining your physical and emotional health is vital for keeping you centred throughout your journey.

Physical health

It is easier to complete your thesis if you stay healthy. Before you begin your thesis writing journey make time to get a full health checkup and try to maintain regular checks along the way. This might take a little time, but it is a great investment in your future. This section of the book focuses on multiple ways of being that can help you stay healthy.

Physical health is affected by many things. This might sound like a parent speaking, but experience speaks the truth of it. Diet plays a significant role in health and feelings of well-being. A thesis requires you to think long and hard. This burns up extra calories but reaching for the chocolate bar or other unhealthy snacks needs to be kept in check. Can you balance your meals out so that they contain at least some healthy food groups to keep the inner self going full steam ahead? Consider your inner identity as a cook. You may like to plan your meals for the week. Think about eating meals with family or friends at least twice a week. You might also think about accepting offers from family and friends for the occasional food hamper. It's easy to miss meals and drink continuous cups of coffee all day as you struggle to put your words on the page.

Physical exercise is important too. We all know that physical exercise is good for your body and helps balance out your emotions, but it can have extra benefits when words are not flowing. You might like to use exercise as a way of temporarily distancing yourself from your research, a kind of thesis timeout. You might like to walk with a friend. Movement, fresh air and gentle stretching help to refresh the body and mind. Or you might want to take up more vigorous exercise as a way of venting frustration after a day of writing. You might find a hidden energy boost from kickboxing and Zumba dancing. Those endorphins can be pretty fun! Think about exercise you do, and how you can keep it part of your routine. Are there any exercises that you would like to take up? Perhaps you can achieve two goals at the same time: write a thesis and learn a sport. Taking time for whatever form of exercise you enjoy the most will keep your thesis moving ahead, especially if you can build it into a routine that you can maintain.

Your physical health is also dependent on what you do when you write your thesis. Think about your physical health while you sit at your computer. Physical well-being is affected by sitting too long and by watching the computer screen for hours on end. Lots of thesis writers have eye strain and back and neck problems when they work long hours on the screen. Make time to get your eyes tested and ensure you have glasses suitable for working with screens. If you are working in a university office, request an appropriate chair and desk. If you regularly write at home, investing in a comfortable and ergonomic chair for your home workspace is by no means an extravagance. If you are employed, this could be a tax deduction, along with your glasses. If not, ask the university if you can have an ergonomic chair for working at home. By considering your workspaces and how it can be better suited to your physical needs, your body will feel better at the end of the day, and you will be fresh to start on your thesis again another day.

Train yourself to take breaks to give yourself a rest. You could set a timer to help you get up and move regularly.

Taking regular short breaks from the computer can be an effective way of moving your thesis forward. Your brain is an excellent multitasker and whirrs away in the background while you peel vegetables for dinner, catch up with friends and family, or throw a load of washing on. A short standup chat with your office mates can also be an effective way of talking about what you are working on so that when you return to it, you have a clearer focus. Please do be mindful of your office mates, though, as they may not be ready for a break when you are.

Emotional health

Writing a thesis can be overwhelming. Maintaining your emotional health is vital. Your thesis will take up but it shouldn't take up all your time. There are practical aspects to managing your emotional health. Maintaining outside interests are crucial to keep your life in balance. Spending time with loved ones recharges your reserves of energy and this refuels your progress. Keep stock of the things you love doing with others, and don't pass up on them. Schedule activities so that you can de-stress. Regular activities will be easier to fit into your schedule, if you plan for them. Even if you might not feel like taking time away from your thesis, breaks from your thesis are a good investment. You will be more on task, and more productive because of them.

Feeling comfortable in your working surroundings is equally important to your emotional health because your office is where you will spend a lot of your time. You might put photos of family within sight of your computer to remind yourself of your centre. Maintaining connection to family and country throughout your thesis is vital for your well-being. These connections provide you with purpose and emotional support when you need it most. Many thesis writers find it available to share their joys about their research experiences. Remember, your thesis is important, there is more to you than your thesis.

Because writing a thesis is so time-consuming, your emotional health depends on your willingness to ask periodically for support. For some of you, this may make you feel uncomfortable. You may need varied sorts of personal help depending on your circumstances – support with the kids, someone to call in on your parents, someone to cook meals … the list will be endless. Having conversations about the need for support before you begin your thesis will make it easier when you do need it. Family and friends may make the offer before you ask. If they offer, accept! They may have detected that you are more stressed than you recognize. Opening up about your emotions with family and friends is useful for sharing your journey. They can't write your thesis, but they might help you stay centred, and more emotionally fit for the journey ahead.

If you don't want to share your feelings with family or friends, the university has free counselling services that provide opportunities for you to vent your pent-up frustrations.

Your emotional health means keeping yourself emotionally centred. If you are someone constantly feeling guilty for not being able to do as much as you did in the past for family or friends, you may try asking for forgiveness. For some, this may be a useful healing process and a way of supporting everyone to move forward.

3. Nurturing your personal relationships

Before you embark on a thesis, reflect on the effects that your thesis journey will have on your relationships with others. How will your thesis affect your work/life and home/life balances? How will others navigate around your thesis? If you change your ways of parenting, child-caring, as well as the time you spend with your partner, and friends, will everyone be okay with the changes? Is this a good time for you to let your thesis get in the way of important interactions with others? For most people, writing a thesis is a totally consuming activity for a relatively long period of time. You and the people around you need to be prepared and willing to take this journey.

For many of you, your family or friendship groups will change in reaction to your new identities of researcher and thesis writer. You will not be able to do all the things that you might have done in the past and others will need to take on additional tasks and sometimes do things without you. Will you and they be comfortable with these outcomes?

When thinking about others, another consideration is time to complete your thesis. How much time do you have to undertake a thesis now? If your family, friends and work need you now more than normal, or if you know there are issues now (stresses at home or at work or with friends and family), perhaps it might be better to leave thesis writing for a year or two. If you can see positive ways of carving out space for thesis writing and are excited by the prospect, then this IS the best time to make that decision and engage in the research journey as no timing will be perfect. We never know the future.

No matter what your plan, expect the thesis journey to be a fluid one. It will change you and those around you in expected and unexpected ways (Barnacle & Mewburn, 2010). While the change will be exciting, it will also be exhausting. It will, in the end, be life-transforming. In an earlier section about you, we asked that you consider nurturing yourself by drawing on the people around you. It is equally vital that you consider how to nurture your existing interactions with friends and family for their sake. Think about having a regular scheduled meal, a date night, a movie night, or anything that everyone regularly enjoys. It's crucial for friends and family that you remain engaged in their lives.

Finally, as a research scholar, you will meet new people, engage in new activities and learn new ways of being and doing. Your interactions in your academic life will affect what you do, where you go and what you talk about. Are you and your family prepared for you to take up new friendships that may not include them?

4. Developing your academic support networks

As a researcher, you are part of a scholarly community. Your scholarly community can be as narrow or as broad as you like. You can engage with colleagues in your discipline, meet regularly with favorite study-buddies, or possibly participate in a writing group. You can join in seminars and attend conferences as well as engage in professional development at your university library or faculty/school/department. Online forums have come to the fore – and were strongly reinforced recently during the COVID-19 pandemic. They offer an alternative medium for support. Engagement in wider academic communities has numerous benefits. This engagement enables stronger academic identities to emerge. This helps keep you inspired and in control. It also provides you with support. Don't think about doing your thesis on your own! If you are shy, and you don't want to join forums where you are required to talk, you can still learn from attending events when sitting quietly in the back of the room.

Enrolling in seminars brings you in contact with emerging researchers and thesis writers like yourself. As a researcher and thesis writer you share a common identity. Having friends who understand at least some of your ways of being and doing can help you through your thesis journey. If your university does not offer classes on research and thesis writing, you may want to seek out other thesis writers to share your journey. The possibilities are endless. Sometimes thesis writers form friendship groups with shared gender, age, religious, geographical or cultural backgrounds. Such friendship groups are often a useful way of discovering that you share similar challenges. Thesis writers can also benefit by interacting with thesis writers from different backgrounds, as their different ways of being can provide useful insights into how to look at the world in a different way. Some of which can open up different ways of seeing the world and how your thesis research fits within it.

Search out and sign up for induction sessions for thesis writers early in your candidature when time constraints are less pressing. Be selective about the sessions you attend because some sessions might serve you better later in your thesis writing journey.

If you want to ensure that you can communicate with a wider audience, participating in writing and discussion groups can be useful. As your researcher identity emerges, your support networks may change. You may find thesis completion workshops useful as you near completion, as you might find you want to be guided in ways to finalize your thesis. Or you may want to assert yourself and get your work known by engaging with a wider academic community through conference participation and publishing. If you are outgoing, you may even volunteer to chair a session, if asked. It is up to you how much or how little you engage with the communities. Each researcher needs to find the right balance for them at the various stages in the thesis journey. But don't be pushed into things you don't believe fit with who you are and don't take on so many things that you forget your main focus. Above all, try not to shy away from taking on any activities that challenge your researcher and thesis writer identity. They are valuable parts of learning.

For more on the importance of engagement in scholarly communities, you might like to read Pyhältö and Keskinen (2012). Carter, Blumenstein and Cook (2013) examine gender implications for identity transformation in doctoral studies, and Aitchison and Mowbray (2013) discuss the complexity involved in managing family relationships and thesis writing. They both illuminate challenges faced by women in managing their multiple identities while writing a thesis.

Notes

1 You may bring sets of skills about accessing support systems that can positively contribute to your thesis journey as well as that of those around you. Everyone needs support at some time, and you may be the person most knowledgeable and best able to provide needed advice to fellow thesis writers.

2 Within the university and other networks, there are many to support you, including ally networks such as First Nations groups, your place of worship, or LGBTQI+ support groups.

3 Being passionate about a topic has been shown to be particularly good for other aspects of your emerging researcher identity. It is particularly useful for building research networks and giving presentations.

References

Aitchison, Claire, & Mowbray, Susan. (2013). Doctoral women: Managing emotions, managing doctoral studies. *Teaching in Higher Education*, *18*(8), 859–870. https://doi.org/10.1080/13562517.2013.827642

Barnacle, Robyn, & Mewburn, Inger. (2010). Learning networks and the journey of 'becoming doctor'. *Studies in Higher Education*, *35*(4), 433–444. https://doi.org/10.1080/03075070903131214

Browne, Kath, & Nash, Catherine J. (2010). *Queer methods and methodologies: Intersecting queer theories and social science research*. Taylor & Francis.

Carter, Susan, et al. (2013). Different for women? The challenges of doctoral studies. *Teaching in Higher Education*, *18*(4), 339–351. https://doi.org/10.1080/13562517.2012.719159

Formentelli, Maicol, & Hajek, John. (2016). Address practices in academic interactions in a pluricentric language: Australian English, American English, and British English. *Pragmatics*, *26*(1), 631–652. https://doi.org/10.1075/prag.26.4.05for

Morley, Clive. (2005). Supervising professional doctorate research is different. In P. Green (Ed.). *Supervising postgraduate research: Contexts and processes, theories and practices* (pp. 106–122). RMIT University Press.

Pyhältö, Kirsi, & Keskinen, Jenni. (2012). Doctoral students' sense of relational agency in their scholarly communities. *International Journal of Higher Education*, *1*(2), 136–149. https://doi.org/10.5430/ijhe.v1n2p136

Nguyet Nguyen, Minh, & Robertson, Margaret J. (2022). International students enacting agency in their PhD journey. *Teaching in Higher Education*, *27*(6), 814–830. https://doi.org/10.1080/13562517.2020.1747423

Singh, Michael, et al. (2016). Mobilising indigenous and non-western theoretic-linguistic knowledge in doctoral education. *Knowledge Cultures*, *4*(1), 56–70.

Smiler, Kirsten. (2016). Building relationships with whānau to develop effective supports for Māori Deaf children. In Taylor-Leech, Kerry and Donna Starks (Eds.) *Doing research within communities*, (96–104). Abington: Routledge.

Wohling, Marc. (2009). The problem of scale in indigenous knowledge: A perspective from northern Australia. *Ecology and Society*, *14*(1), 1–14. [online] http://www.ecologyandsociety.org/vol14/iss1/art/

Understanding your identities as a researcher, supervisee, and thesis writer

Overview

While the previous chapter was primarily about understanding who you are and preparing for the journey ahead, this chapter considers three key identities that emerge during the journey: those of a researcher, a supervisee and a thesis writer. Each of these identities is associated with distinct ways of knowing, being and doing. Researchers have different views about the world and investigate topics from different perspectives, supervisees see themselves in different ways and work differently in an academic context. Thesis writers have different ways of thinking about themselves as writers and different ways of putting thoughts together to make a compelling text. Understanding what researching, writing and supervision means for you and how you identify in these spheres helps avoid feelings that you are not on the right track just because you are doing things differently. Such understandings are a vital step to completing a successful thesis.

Chapter 3 provides ten pointers to help you understand your emerging identities as a researcher, supervisee and thesis writer. The first of these pointers consider researcher identities, how they differ, their shared commonalities, and what a researcher identity might mean for you. The next couple of pointers in this chapter explore your identities as a supervisee, your preferences and expectations for a supervisor, and your ideas about the best ways to structure supervision sessions. The remaining pointers delve into potential thesis writer identities: whether and how much of your personal identities you might wish to embed into your thesis, how to deal with revisions and what you can learn from examining your supervisor's writing

DOI: 10.4324/9781003323402-3

style. Our final pointer looks at changes to your thesis writer identity at different points in the thesis journey.

Figure 3.1   Juggling your identities

5. Your emerging researcher identities

Undertaking a thesis means going through many transitions and taking on many new identities. This pointer explores one of these – your researcher identities. As aspects of your researcher identity are often influenced by your personal interests, you can gain some initial insights into your identity as a researcher by reflecting on your characteristic conversations with others. Do you like to discuss practical issues, deeper policy debates, or do you like to focus on words, what they mean and how they are used? By actively contemplating the macro-issues that interest you, you can come to know the kind of research that best suits you.

You can also think about your identities as a researcher by considering the preferred types of data. Is your interest piqued when others discuss numbers, or do you prefer to listen to stories that people tell? Your personal preferences can help you decide whether to undertake a large-scale quantitative investigation or a case study investigating the experiences of a single person or organization.

Your personal preferences as a researcher can also influence how you complete your thesis – whether you want to complete a thesis solely by writing a volume of text or through other means, such as creating a documentary. When your ways of being and doing in life are in sync with those in your thesis, it helps keep you focused and motivated during your thesis journey. It can also give you greater control over your thesis.

While the above discussion asks you to think about different researcher identities, there are commonalities shared amongst researchers in the ways that they go about their work. For some of you, these ways of doing may be challenging to develop. A researcher is someone who can work independently. As a researcher, you will be expected to take charge of your own professional development: to learn new skills that you require for your thesis journey without being told to do so.[1] There are expectations that you will take control of your time management and not get distracted by enrolling in too many workshops or other activities. If you find this daunting, talk to other thesis writers about how they manage and have an honest conversation with your supervisor(s) early in your candidature about how you can best proceed.

Another part of a researcher identity is embracing a reading culture. The amount of required reading can catch some thesis writers by surprise. To become an 'expert' in one small area, you will actively read extensively, often beyond readings suggested by your supervisor(s). You read for weeks or months before you write anything. This may make you feel like you are not making any progress and that the supervisor is not letting you get on with the thesis. In some instances, you may read extensively only to realize that your way of exploring your topic has been researched and that you must start a new reading cycle on another topic. In the process of reading, you may also find that you are not truly interested in the topic and want to explore something new. This is a heartbreaking part of being a researcher and happens to quite a few of us. If you have any of these experiences, you may need friends and family to provide you with emotional support (see Chapter 2 for details). It is important that you have ongoing conversations with your supervisor(s) about how your topic is progressing, and any changes that you might be considering. Some changes may prompt really good ideas.

Still another part of being a researcher is the demonstration of your newly acquired knowledge. Within this demonstration of knowledge, there is an expectation that you will create your own positioning within the argument being made, and that you will develop the courage to state what you think and why. A vital step for any researcher is the development of a critical reading identity (Hammond, 2022), an identity that is of importance to all researchers. As a researcher, you are expected to process what you read and constantly question all aspects of it. For some researchers, this takes practice. For some of you, the content in some of your readings may sometimes conflict with some of your ways of knowing, being and doing. Your researcher identity may question what you may have assumed as cultural or religious truths. You may need to lean on fellow thesis writers to give you strength. You can seek advice from researchers who share similar personal backgrounds for ideas about how to demonstrate knowledge in ways that fit with your identity.

Still another key part of a researcher identity involves the way that you react to feedback. A researcher identity is one that views feedback as useful. For many emerging researchers, addressing extensive cycles of feedback can be challenging. This may be the first time that you have experienced detailed critiques of this kind. While you may pride yourself on your research, you may feel that your supervisory team is constantly discovering holes in your argument and argumentation. You will learn to work with cycles of feedback rather than against them (see Pointer 43 in Chapter 6). Supervisors have a strong interest in the development of your researcher identity. They are only trying to make your work better. As a researcher, you embrace critique; it empowers critical thinking.

Finally, as a researcher, you see yourself as a member of a supervisory team – one that includes you and your supervisor(s). Your entire supervisory team (or you and your supervisor if you are an honors or minor thesis student) is trying to help you fine-tune what you have to say so that you project a strong researcher identity: one that demonstrates that you have read widely, that you have an argument to make, and that you can back up your claims with solid evidence. As a supervisory team you all want to work together to portray information clearly and concisely. They will help you achieve this.

While some things that your supervisor(s) say will make immediate sense to you and you will willingly treasure this feedback and use it in your future ways of doing, you may not understand why other revisions are necessary. This may leave you feeling confused and disheartened. Ask for clarification if you don't understand any suggested changes. If you don't understand the feedback, you won't be able to evaluate its usefulness and you won't be able to work together as a team.

6. Planning for your professional self – post degree

In the transformative process of completing the thesis, both you and your ideas change. With change, it may be easy to lose your sense of purpose. So, it is useful to stop and ponder your final intended outcome. For some, your thesis might mark an end for your research career. That is totally fine. A thesis can simply be a something that you wanted to do for the sake of doing it. Go for it!

Others of you may be thinking about your future and where a thesis might lead. In many cases, you may not be entirely sure. If you are thinking about something that involves research, it is useful to keep careful track of any accrued research skills from your thesis journey. These might include acquired skills around library research, data collection and analysis, critical research and reasoning, grant and report writing skills. These skills are all highly prized in industry and government, as well as in universities. By keeping track of your skillsets and where and when you obtained them, you can gradually prepare your CV for when you are ready for that next job. With a well-prepared CV, your researcher identity can easily be directed at developing a new research identity, a 'future self' (Bentley et al., 2019).

If you are thinking about the thesis to procure a particular research job, you may like to scout out employment advertisements and target your thesis to investigate specific issues mentioned in job descriptions and their selection criteria. This will increase your chances of future employment success. You might like to approach potential employers for an internship or see if they offer scholarships in or around your research topic. Focused internships and scholarships can provide a foothold in the profession. If you are looking for future work in the community sphere, you might like to spend time volunteering to become known in the community. Volunteering has additional benefits. As a researcher, you have valuable knowledge and experience to share. Volunteering can give you access to friendly faces who are interested in listening to your thesis topic because your topic has relevance to them.

Some of you may already have a job that you enjoy, and you may see your thesis as a key part of your career progression. You may wish to return to your existing job, or potentially aspire to a different job in the same company. Completing your thesis can create useful pathways to the next stage of your life. If your thesis is for career advancement, your thesis topic can be a vital part of that career path. It is not unusual for those coming from industry to use the thesis as an opportunity to address industry-related issues. Perhaps you can use research ideas from your thesis to enact changes to practices in your field, and perhaps get a promotion in the process. If this is your thesis pathway, when choosing your thesis topic, think carefully about whether any potential results will be ones that your employer may not like to hear, or have published. Think about what you might do under such circumstances. If you are uncomfortable with this possibility, you might like to talk to your employer before embarking on your thesis.

Another option is to see your thesis as a pathway to an academic career. There is much preparation needed for this highly competitive career pathway. While completing your thesis, you may want to spend energy on networking at conferences to get noticed in the world of academia. You may spend time attending grant-writing seminars, so that you have grants to list in your curriculum vitae. You may apply for part-time tutoring to establish a teaching identity. You might want to publish a paper or two from your thesis before you submit your thesis so that you have publications. You might even consider completing a thesis by/with publication (see Pointer 24 for details). Such an approach is likely to help you develop stronger links with your supervisor(s) and help you obtain a stronger letter of reference. Think carefully about what you hope to achieve and how you might best manage your time to achieve it. It is easy to get sidelined from your research if you take on too much.

For further reading you might like to read the collection of accounts from past graduates in Maureen Ryan (2012). The graduates discuss their professional experiences, influences on the transformation of their professional identities, topic choices and managing life as a student.

7. Seeing yourself as a supervisee: your requirements for a supervisor

Thesis writers face the contradiction of having to negotiate the demands of being an independent reader and thinker within the context of being supervised by others.[2] This dualism means that being supervised doesn't come easily. This requires the supervisory team to work together to develop a productive relationship to achieve the best supervision possible. It is important that your supervisor is someone who you can depend on for advice and support and with whom you can comfortably collaborate. But what does that really mean? You might start by thinking about you and your existing skillset. For theses in social sciences (humanities, education, business, law, creative arts etc.), your topic may be personal, and you may bring funds of knowledge with you. If you are a highly skilled and knowledgeable professional in a particular area, you may need to look around for someone interested in your topic and interested in learning from you. If you know little about the topic, you may need an expert in your chosen area. Alternatively, you may feel that you can handle the topic but need help with theory or methodology. Or perhaps you might like an all-rounder who may not be an expert in your chosen area but can help you in other ways such as time management, academic writing and so on.

World views matter too. It is best to find supervisors who are open to your world view. For example, if you come from a social justice world view, you may find it a constant challenge to work with supervisors who think within a neoliberal rational economic framework. While the challenge of working with supervisors who have a radically different perspective could excite you, you might also find it exhausting.

Your ways of being and doing also require some consideration, be they cultural, gender or age-based, or the result of your physical disabilities. All can affect your interaction with your supervisor(s). A supervisor doesn't need to be the same as you, but it is useful to talk with any supervisor(s) about your ways of being and doing at the start of your thesis to ensure compatibility. If you have specific needs (such as the use of a neopronoun [see Pointer 37 on gendered pronouns] or a specially set up audio loop, or you require supervision outside of regular working hours), how willing are your supervisor(s) to work around your needs? You won't know if you don't ask.

Effective communication is crucial in strong supervision teams. Talking through communication protocols early in supervision is a useful strategy. Work out issues such as timelines for sending and receiving work for feedback. You might also like to think about how to best structure your communication in your supervision sessions. Are you someone who likes to come in with topics to discuss? Do you like to debate concepts, or do you like to avoid conflict, listening and doing what others suggest? Do you want someone to guide you every step of the way or someone who will leave you free to explore on your own? Supervision works best when you and your supervisors understand each other.

Your views about what is involved in supervision also require some thought. Some supervisors separate research from daily life; some do not. Do you prefer a supervisor who takes a hands-off approach from your personal life or a supervisor who takes a wholistic approach to supervision and approaches you and your thesis with high levels of emotional caring? Would you be comfortable having a regular meeting agenda item that checks on the health of your supervisor–supervisee working relationships to ensure that everyone is managing comfortably? Would your supervisor(s) be comfortable with this? Perhaps you should ask.

In some circumstances, you may have to give your supervisor a 'heads up' if you need to adjust your timeline to account for issues at home or work. Regular communication with your supervisors is the bedrock of good progress.[3] Discussing your progress (and any setbacks you may be experiencing) could be a topic of your supervisory meetings every couple of months, or a more regular but very brief discussion at the beginning of every session. This might be five minutes when things are not going well and one or two minutes at times when everything is going smoothly.

Some of you may have very specific requirements for selecting your supervisors. Carter, Laurs, Chant & Wolfgramm-Foliaki (2018) provide insights into how to engage with indigenous cultural identities in supervisory contexts. Collins (2015) provides useful commentary on supervisory issues for those who have additional learning needs.

8. Seeing yourself as a supervisee: assessing your requirements for supervision sessions

We all manage our time differently. Some people like tight schedules and regular meetings with predetermined agenda items and some do not. The nature of supervision sessions depends on the people in them. You may like to meet with your supervisor(s) on a regular basis, or only when you ready to present work and receive feedback. Many thesis writers are somewhere between the two points. You may prefer some flexibility yet at the same time, some structure to ensure that you meet regularly (whatever that may mean for you).

When thinking about your supervision meetings, think about who you are and how flexible you need to be to fulfil your thesis commitments. Do you think you might like drop-in meetings for a quick chat rather than regular-length bi-weekly or monthly meeting? Are you happy to meet online always, or sometimes is face-to-face essential for you? With our ever-evolving world, you may not always have a choice, but think about your preferences and make those preferences clear in your discussions with your potential supervisor(s). Think about their general availability as well. High profile researchers tend to spend more time presenting their research overseas and may not be able to have regularly scheduled meetings. More junior research-ers tend to be around a lot more.

There are also different ways to how to run a supervision session. Do you prefer highly structured meetings or ones that vary from one meeting to the next (e.g., one meeting on writing and one on content)?

In your supervision sessions, do you prefer to work with all the team all the time,[4] would you be comfortable to alternate meetings between the supervisor and co-supervisor (if you have one), or do you prefer to work with the principal supervisor and keep the other supervisor briefed? Perhaps you like group supervision where you can learn from the ways that other thesis writers do things. You may not know until you experience these options. You might like to ask your supervisor(s) about how they feel on these issues.

Many universities ask for you to run through a checklist with your supervisor(s) in the first couple of months of candidature, but you might like to discuss ways of being and doing even before you start. Discussing your meet-ing preferences within your supervisory team is a wise strategy. Supervisors often have their own ways of being and doing but are often open to alternative ways when you bring them to the discussion early in your candidature.

Once you settle on your supervisor(s) and discuss arrangements for work-ing together, you may want to document it. You may find it much easier to raise concerns if things are not going as well as hoped. Be prepared to adjust as you go though. Circumstances will most likely change for all individuals in the team, especially if your thesis journey spans multiple years. For further details, see Chapter 6.

Effective supervision has been identified as the single biggest factor in successful completion (DeClercq et al., 2019), so spend time building your supervisory team. If you are writing a doctoral thesis, connections with your supervisor(s) can last many years. A good relationship with your supervisor(s) may well transfer to long term professional relationships that include co-authoring post thesis.

If you want to read further about different ways of working within supervision teams, you can read through stories that elaborate on responses to different working arrangements in Robertson (2019). For a more conceptual discussion of team supervision, you might prefer Robertson (2017). Broder Sumerson (2013) has some great advice on setting up your supervision committee, and approaches to help you move forward in the academic world.

9. Developing your thesis writer identities

Your unique ways of knowing, being and doing inevitably affect how you write your thesis. No two thesis writers are the same. Sometimes the differences are obvious to all. Your topic, theoretical framings and methodological positionings come to mind here. Sometimes, differences are more subtle, embedded into your thesis through the ways that you connect with your text. In the remainder of this chapter, we ask you to spend a little time to think about who you are and how you might want to write yourself into your thesis (if at all).

There are multiple ways in which you can bring yourself into your thesis. You might think about questions such as: Are you happy to tell a personal story about yourself to show what your topic means to you? Are you comfortable giving examples from your personal and academic life to support your academic argument? Do you see yourself as a participant in your study and, if so, how much information are you going to provide about yourself when describing your participants? How much of your analysis are you going to 'admit' may have influenced your interpretation based on your background? We consider these and other related issues in Chapter 4.

A second type of question to consider is how important it is to write in ways that reflect your ways of expression. In Chapter 1 we raised the idea that writing is not 'faceless'. The ways you analyze how you write says a lot about you. Are you someone who is overly comfortable adopting writing conventions that resemble academic textbook English because you feel that the advice improves your ways of writing? Or do you take on writing advice because this is what you have been told that you should do even though it doesn't feel like you? If you accept thesis writing advice that does not sound like who you are and/or who you would like to be, you will have difficulty writing in that way. Think about how you wish to project a powerful voice in your writing – one that sounds like the authentic 'you'. It may be difficult, but it will be worth it in the end. See Chapters 4 and 5 for some thoughts on potential possibilities.

You may want to consider Canagarajah's (2022) recent article on expressing yourself in and through your text and some of the difficulties multilinguals face in crafting text. Although Canagarajah's article was written with multilingual writers in mind, it has useful insights if you wish to portray your identities through the ways that you write – even if you only use one language.

10. Are you prepared for the writing journey? Your initial drafts

To be prepared for the writing journey, it is also vital to reflect on how you engage in the writing process. If you are someone who likes to write a very clean text in their first draft, you are likely to spend a long time thinking about your ideas before you write them or a long time writing up your ideas before you are willing to let your supervisor(s) see them. Writing in this way provides your supervisor(s) with a clean, clear text. It is much easier for supervisors to provide feedback when the text reads well. But this kind of writing process also has downsides. You may not be good at making deadlines and this may affect your ability to complete your thesis on time (see Chapter 6 for details). Other serious issues may arise. You may be so dedicated to your writing that you may not wish to discard the text if your supervisor suggests you try another very different approach to the topic or asks you to reorganize your ideas. You may feel reluctant to engage in change. Your supervisor(s) need insights into your thinking as it develops. This is the only way that they can understand where you are going (and why). If you spend too much time refining ideas before you have discussed them with your supervisor(s), you may have to rewrite everything all over again. This can be truly disheartening.

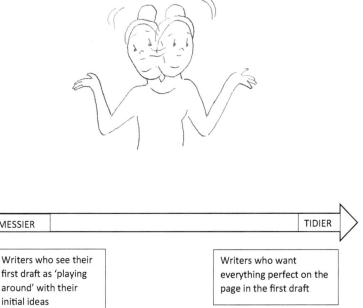

(a)

MESSIER		TIDIER

Writers who see their first draft as 'playing around' with their initial ideas	Writers who want everything perfect on the page in the first draft

(b)

Figure 3.2   Where do you fit as a thesis writer on the tidiness scale?

If you are *not* someone who is deeply invested in perfect text in your first draft, you may be more resilient to requests for major rewrites. If you see your draft chapters as needing improvement, you may set yourself up to be more willing to engage in a constructive dialogue that enhances your thinking and writing and moves your writing forward. However, this approach also has downsides. If your initial drafts are too untidy, your supervisors may not be able to understand your claims and may get frustrated with your grammar, spelling mistakes, etc. This may mean that they cannot focus on the content. Most supervisors find it very difficult to read untidy texts, especially when they are rushed for time. If the supervisor is a very tidy writer, there may be an expectation that you will write in similar ways.

If you are someone who likes to simply get words on the page as a way of starting ideas or someone who finds the revision process frustrating, you may want to suggest to your supervisor(s) that you present your initial ideas as a short Power Point presentation, or as a mind-map (see Wette, 2017). This will help you to construct ideas before you spend time crafting the sentences. By writing text only when your arguments and concepts are clear, you can avoid spending time creating well-formulated sentences or paragraphs which may not lead anywhere.

11. Are you prepared for the writing journey? Revisions

Being prepared for revision can help you deal with it. For some researchers, it isn't the extensive time that it takes to conduct the research that causes thesis writer anxiety – it's the revision process. You need to be mentally prepared to not only work on a piece of writing for months on end, but also be prepared to start over again.

The drafts will pile up. There can be multiple drafts as you struggle with how to frame your initial ideas on the page. Then comes a stage where you shape those ideas into a finely-tuned argument. This stage usually requires further drafts. There will be other revisions when you connect the parts together to form a complete chapter and again at the end, when you ensure that all the bits of the thesis fit together. A thesis writer needs persistence.

While most thesis writers struggle with the revision process, others can struggle letting things go. As with any creative pursuit, there comes a point where you begin to overwork the piece. You may become so anxious about having every word and phrase perfect that you fear moving on. You must at some point let go. Perfection is an unobtainable goal. Rather, the aim is for near perfection.

For further insights, Bolke (1998) gives a range of advice and support for your writing journey. A more recent article by Mochizuki and Starfield (2021) provides useful glimpses into the benefits of developing your authorial voice through dialogue. The authors emphasize how talking about your writing can help you with your thinking (and ultimately your writing process).

12. Are you prepared for the thesis writing journey? Patience

There are a few things that you can do to avoid countless revisions. A successful thesis writer has patience, carefully explaining each key point so that your supervisor(s) does not have to dig deep into their memory to fill in details. Clearly documenting all steps in your thinking makes it easier for your supervisor(s) to follow what you want to say. A patient writer helps their supervisor(s) understand the text.

Clearly articulating all steps of your thinking in your writing fulfils an additional purpose; it helps you present the 'facts' as you want them presented. When this happens, your supervisor(s) start to think in the way that you want them to think. As you take your supervisor(s) through your thinking, draw attention to those ideas that you believe to be important. Retell the key points as you see them. When you consider your writing as a retelling experience, you are also less likely to bog your supervisor(s) down with needless details or present excessive information not related to 'your' key points.

There are a multitude of writing strategies that you can use to guide your reader, many outlined in Chapter 5. The key point behind all these strategies is that you need to take time to guide your reader in the direction that you want them to go. It's important not to jump to the next point before fully exploring the first one. A patient thesis writer guides their supervisor slowly and carefully so that your text and its intended direction are understood. To best achieve this goal, you need to patiently articulate all your ideas. This is the first of many steps in developing an authoritative author voice.

For further ideas on the nature of voice in thesis writing, Morton and Storch's (2019) article is a useful start.

13. How useful is it to replicate your supervisor's style?

Because each person is different, there is no one 'correct' way to write a thesis. If you share similar writing styles to your supervisor(s), you will likely have less heated discussions about how to write. But if you don't write like your supervisor(s), it's not the end of the world. It is more important to know what your differences are so that you can articulate why you write as you do.

To get insights into how your writer identity might differ from other members of your supervisory team, you may want to do a little side research. An analysis of recent work is a useful strategy.[5] How do your supervisor(s) structure their text? In journal articles, do they have long detailed introductions that survey the history of the field, or do they survey only literature that is of direct relevance to their topic? Do they state the research question at the beginning of their papers, at the end of the introduction, or wait until they get to the methodology? Are their discussions summary-like (e.g., they stick with the facts), or do they use their conclusions to explore tentative ideas? Are their conclusions brief, or long? If long, what kinds of things do they include/exclude? Do they use personal pronouns in their writing? Are their sentences long or short? Would you naturally structure your text in the same way? Do you like their writing style? Would you be comfortable writing this way? As a little writing exercise, take a couple of abstracts your supervisors have written and put them into your own words. What differences do you see?

Through exploring differences, you will learn a few useful tricks of the trade. But remember that not everyone writes in the same way and if you try to mindlessly replicate the ways that others write, you may find that you lose part of your identity in the process. Some changes will feel good for you, others may not.

In the end, you will undoubtedly take on some aspects of your supervisor(s)' writing styles, you will reject some others, even meld varied pieces thereof with your ways of writing. You may even find that some writing styles that you rejected early in your thesis journey are embraced later as you see things in a different light. Some aspects that you embraced early on may be rejected as you establish your own identity in the field as a researcher and thesis writer. You will change during your thesis journey, and this will affect some of the ways that you write.

You can think about the ways your supervisor writes and how it compares with your own writing style without discussing this with your supervisor. However, if you want to write your thesis in ways that disrupt conventional discourse (a documentary, a play, a conversation – the options are endless), and this is not the typical genre for your supervisor(s), have a forthright discussion in your supervisory team around your thoughts about this before embarking on your writing journey.

There are many successful examples of theses written that disrupt conventional discourse. Weatherall (2019) describes how she used queer theory in the field of management to write a non-conventional thesis. You might find this work helpful as a way of thinking about writing outside of the norm. In her work, rather than separating theoretical material from data detailing the experiences of her participants, she wove the two together as a narrative to enable her to write her emotional responses to her data. Although we don't know for sure, we suspect that this thesis option required considerable discussion with her supervisors.

14. Engaging further with imagined researcher and thesis writer identities

There are other identities that intersect with, overlap and transcend researcher and thesis writer identities. One of these is the identity of the academic. As a researcher, you may or may not identify as an academic depending on how you see your research and your work life. As a thesis writer, you may see yourself as a particular type of academic based on your thoughts about your ways of being and doing. At different times in your thesis journey, you are likely to see yourself as more or less of an academic, researcher, and thesis writer. In times of self-doubt (see Pointer 42), you may not see yourself as any of the above.

Your researcher and thesis writer identities change throughout your thesis journey. At the beginning of your thesis, you may see your researcher and thesis writer identities as emerging. In other words, you may not view yourself as an expert researcher or thesis writer. After you have completed multiple workshops and read hundreds of documents you are likely to begin to see yourself as an expert in APA7 or some other referencing style. After you have defended/confirmed your thesis proposal, you may see yourself as someone who can give advice to those thesis writers who are not yet at that stage. When you have received glowing examiners' reports, you may even begin to see yourself as an expert in your topic. Other identities (i.e., a careful researcher, helpful academic, and critical reader identities) will similarly morph over time. You will gradually develop an identity as a more confident thesis writer.

Throughout your thesis journey, your identities interact. Your researcher and thesis writer identities will sometimes be in sync with your personal ways of being and doing. If you are someone who is usually careful and cautious, then you may find it easy to develop cautious and careful researcher and thesis writer identities. If you are someone who is normally helpful, your researcher and thesis writer identities may also benefit from these aspects of your personal identity. If you have an existing identity as a good communicator, this may make it easier to talk to others about your work as you write your thesis. Some of your personal ways of being may affect how you write your thesis. If you have strong national identity, you may choose topics about where you are from and write in ways that convey that message. You might even like to check up on geographical differences in English language use (see Pointer 38 for things that normally don't matter that much).

Not everything will be in sync, and it doesn't have to be. Some of your existing personal ways of being and doing will conflict with your emerging identities as you become a confident researcher and thesis writer. As you change, keep in mind that change is not unidirectional. Your emerging identities as a researcher and thesis writer can influence ways of being and doing in your personal life. As an example, Starks and Nicholas' (2020) report on how some Vietnamese masters' students noticed that their academic identities as writers of academic English influenced how they now write (and sometimes think) in everyday encounters in Vietnamese.

In the next two chapters, we shift from a focus on identities to explore various ways that you perform those identities through the ways that you write your thesis. The aim here is to enable you to perform a thesis writer identity that makes you sound (to you and potentially others) as confident, careful, helpful and tidy thesis writer who sees themselves as an expert in at least one small area of study. As each thesis writer is different, there are no set rules. There are multiple ways to go about writing your thesis. The pointers in Chapters 4 and 5 aim to provide you with ideas to help you to start to conceptualize your writing journey. Chapter 4 covers macro-topics, such as how to write your introductory chapter, while Chapter 5 focuses on how to transform smaller parts of your text to make you sound like a confident thesis writer in ways that fit with your ways of being and doing.

Notes

1 Look for available workshops at your university library and in your graduate school. If there is workshop that you feel you need but it isn't available, ask. They may be able to offer something if you ask.
2 We would like to thank Howard Nicholas for this idea.
3 Talking with your supervisor about your well-being might include discussions about family issues and even things like crashing your car or dealing with speeding fines.
4 Different university systems have different arrangements for supervision. Most often, honors and master's supervision are undertaken by a single supervisor. For doctoral studies, there is often a supervisory team, with an additional supervisor acting as an advisor to the principal supervisor, and an impartial chair who is

often outside the discipline. In the USA and Canada, the supervisory team is typically conceived of as a supervision panel that supports the principal supervisor; in Australia, United Kingdom, and New Zealand, the principal and co-supervisors tend to share more of the supervision.

5 Your supervisors' writing identities have adapted over time, as they reacted to editor and reviewer comments about their work. Learning to write is a life-long process; it changes over time. Read something recent that your supervisor has written.

References

Bentley, Sarah V., et al. (2019). Construction at work: Multiple identities scaffold professional identity development in academia. *Frontiers in Psychology*, *10*(628), 1–13. https://doi.org/10.3389/fpsyg.2019.00628

Bolke, Joan. (1998). *Writing your thesis in 15 minutes a day: A guide to starting, revising and finishing your doctoral thesis*. Henry Holt.

Canagarajah, Suresh. (2022). Language diversity in academic writing: Toward decolonizing scholarly publishing. *Journal of Multicultural Discourses*, *17*(2), 107–128. https://doi.org/10.1080/17447143.2022.2063873

Carter, Susan, et al. (2018). Indigenous knowledges and supervision: Changing the lens. *Innovations in Education and Teaching International*, *55*(3), 384–393. https://doi.org/10.1080/14703297.2017.1403941

Collins, Bethan. (2015). Reflections on doctoral supervision: Drawing from the experiences of students with additional learning needs in two universities. *Teaching in Higher Education*, *20*(6), 587–600. https://doi.org/10.1080/13562517.2015.1045859

De Clercq, Mikaël, et al. (2019). I need somebody to lean on. *Swiss Journal of Psychology*. https://doi.org/10.1024/1421-0185/a000224

Hammond, Michael. (2022). *Writing a postgraduate thesis or dissertation: Tools for success*. Taylor & Francis.

Mochizuki, Naoko, & Starfield, Sue. (2021). Dialogic interactions and voice negotiations in thesis writing groups: An activity systems analysis of oral feedback exchanges. *Journal of English for Academic Purposes*, *50*. https://doi.org/10.1016/j.jeap.2020.100956

Morton, Janne, & Storch, Neomy. (2019). Developing an authorial voice in PhD multilingual student writing: The reader's perspective. *Journal of Second Language Writing*, *43*, 15–23. https://doi.org/10.1016/j.jslw.2018.02.004

Robertson, Margaret J. (2017). Team modes and power: Supervision of doctoral students. *Higher Education Research & Development*, *36*(2), 358–371. https://doi.org/10.1080/07294360.2016.1208157

Robertson, Margaret J. (2019). *Power and doctoral supervision teams: Developing team building skills in collaborative doctoral research*. Routledge.

Ryan, Maureen. (Ed.). (2012). *Reflections on learning, life and work: Completing doctoral studies in mid and later life and career*. Springer.

Starks, Donna, & Nicholas, Howard. (2020). Reflections of Vietnamese English language educators on their writer identities in English and Vietnamese. *Journal of Language, Identity, and Education, 19(3)*, 179–192. https://doi.org/10.1080/153 48458.2019.1655423

Sumerson, Joanne Broder. (2013). *Finish your dissertation, don't let it finish you!*. John Wiley & Sons.

Weatherall, Ruth. (2019). Writing the doctoral thesis differently. *Management Learning, 50*(1), 100–113. https://doi.org/10.1177/1350507618799867

Wette, Rosemary. (2017). Using mind maps to reveal and develop genre knowledge in a graduate research course. *Journal of Second Language Writing, 38*, 58–71. http://dx.doi.org/10.1016/j.jslw.2017.09.005

Organizing the larger pieces of your thesis

Overview

Chapter 4 explores the macro-structure of your thesis and shows how you can take greater control over how you want to be perceived as a thesis writer/researcher. Your choices range from writing yourself into your thesis as an active participant to backgrounding your voice to appear as an impartial observer, to everything in-between.

Goffman (1959, reprinted 2022) wrote about how we need to consider the world as a stage on which we present our various identities. Your thesis is one such stage from which you can perform different ways of being through different ways of doing. If we apply Goffman's dramaturgical perspective to your thesis, you we could argue that you draw on multiple personal, researcher and thesis writer identities at different places in your thesis. Sometimes, your performances on your thesis stage will come easily to you; at other times you may struggle. Sometimes, conflicts and self-doubts can arise as your personal ways of being and doing conflict with thesis performances, making you feel like you are standing in opposition to yourself. Sometimes difficulties arise because your identities differ greatly from other actors on your thesis stage, such as your supervisor(s). If this happens, as a team you might need extensive (and ongoing) dialogue to discover how to write a strong effective thesis that works for you that also connects with those around you.

In Chapter 4, we invite you to look at potential macro-structures for your thesis and how you can write yourself into the various parts of your thesis. We consider ten pointers that you can use to help you think about ways of organizing your thesis. These pointers cover issues from how you might

DOI: 10.4324/9781003323402-4

construct your acknowledgements and introduction to how you might develop your key terms and central ideas. The pointers explore how to bring yourself into your methodology and your findings, as well as how your thesis conclusion and references reflect your membership in your research community. The chapter ends with a discussion of writing a thesis by/with publication[1] to help you decide whether this is a thesis format option you might like to pursue or avoid entirely. All choices are yours to make.

Figure 4.1   Building your thesis

15. Your front matter

Most theses start with front matter: a title, an abstract and a table of contents. This is all a basic template, right? Well, not really. While a title announces to the world what your thesis is about, it also sends initial messages to your audience about you through the ways that it is constructed. Your title can vary in length. It can be a single line, or two or three lines in length. The length of your thesis title projects an image of you as a thesis writer: as someone who likes to detail the message or as someone who likes to focus on the point. The wording of the title can also project an impression of you. Do you want to project a researcher identity in your thesis as someone who is writing for a specialist audience or a broader audience? A title that contains technical terminology projects a different image of the author than a title written entirely in plain language. Your title can also differ in its tone. It can project a serious identity or a lighter one.[2] It can also set the tone for the rest of the thesis.

The abstract is another place where you bring yourself into the thesis. An abstract is a brief synopsis of your thesis, typically its aims, methods, findings, and their implications and significance. While the requirements for an abstract can appear very structured, there is still a lot of flexibility as to where you place your focus. By concentrating on some areas more than others, you let your readers know what is important to you. The way that the text is composed also says a great deal about how you relate to your audience. Does your abstract invite a large readership into your world, or is it written in highly technical language directed at a few specialists in the field?

The table of contents also creates an impression of you as a thesis writer. Are you someone who likes to file thoughts neatly into boxes, numbering headings, subheadings, sub-sub-headings, and even sub-sub-sub-headings? Or are you someone who likes to keep the content more open, with fewer section subheadings? Are you someone who sees the table of contents only as a filing system for the major parts of the thesis, or are you someone who likes to devise your chapter and section headings in ways that tell an initial story about the content of your thesis? Whatever your decisions, when you pull your table of contents together, the structure and wording of your table of contents is your initial story to your reader when they first open your work. For further details on chapter and section headings, see Pointer 25.

Another type of front matter is your acknowledgements. Do you want the acknowledgements to be short or a couple of pages? Do you want its content to appear factual, or do you want to lighten it up? What style of English do you want to use? Many supervisors edit acknowledgements minimally, so this part of your thesis tends to say a lot about your writing practices and the role of support networks in your thesis journey. It alerts the reader to what they might expect throughout your thesis. Examiners may or may not read your acknowledgements, but if they do, they will form a view of you as a person (Kumar & Sanderson, 2020). As this part of your thesis says a lot about you, you should proofread your acknowledgements carefully to ensure that your acknowledgements are grammatically correct and free of typographical errors. You don't want to set up your readers to think that they need to endure numerous typological errors throughout your thesis.

In the acknowledgements, there are lots of people that you want to thank. You might want to consider the order in which you thank your supervisors, your community, your participants, and your friends and family. Who is thanked first (or last) says a lot about how you see their part in your research. Other important decisions include whether to start your introduction with an acknowledgement to country. Do you want to acknowledge the land upon which you wrote/were born/grew up, or only people? What do you want to say about the land, and have you consulted on the appropriateness of this message? Have you thought about the people who you acknowledge who you cannot identify because of ethical constraints, and how you will acknowledge them? If English is not your first language or the first language of the people you are researching, do you thank certain people in your acknowledgement in a language other than English? While your university might not allow you to use a language other than English in the body of your thesis, your acknowledgements are a place where you can identify as multilingual.

For hints about ways to construct parts of your front matter, you might want to look at any early article by Kaplan et al. (1994) on writing an abstract and a later article by Abdel Salam El-Dakhs (2018) on differences between abstracts in doctoral theses and those in research articles. Another useful work for your front matter is Hyland's (2004) analysis of written acknowledgements to theses.

16. Your introduction

Any how-to-write-a-thesis guidebook will tell you that an introductory chapter to a thesis sets the stage for the rest of the work. The chapter contains information about what the thesis is about and why this knowledge is of value for your field of study. This is not an easy chapter to write. So, if you are anxious about your thesis and not entirely sure about its direction, you could consider leaving your introductory chapter until you have a firmer understanding of where the thesis is going and what you want to achieve. If you are someone who must have a finished draft of a chapter before moving on to the next chapter, don't give yourself a case of writer's block. You can write something short and generic to fill in the space. This draft needn't be something that necessarily is shown to your supervisor(s). Most supervisors are fully aware that your introductory chapter is an executive summary that can only be fully written after the thesis is complete. They are often very happy to start with the literature review as this is the chapter that informs your understanding of the field and the research question that you want to address.

Once you are ready to start writing your introduction, consider where you fit. It is your thesis after all. Although there are those who are writing a thesis because their supervisors have suggested a topic, even then you need to have some sort of personal connection with the topic to sustain you through the thesis journey. That interest may be simply because you noticed an intriguing gap in the literature, a gap that enticed you to investigate it further, or it might be much more.

When you are ready to write your introduction, there are options to consider in how you write your identity into this chapter. Like everything in a thesis, you can bring yourself into your introductory chapter in many ways. You may find it helpful to start your thesis with a personal story about you and how you came to be interested in the topic that you are investigating. This is the approach that we have used in our introductory chapter to this book. This type of personalized introduction has the benefit of grounding you to continue your thesis on days when you may feel like giving up. However, it is not for everyone. Starting with a story can be quite unnerving if you are someone who believes that the thesis is an objective scientific piece of writing.[3]

Another way that you can put yourself into your introductory chapter is to illustrate one or more points using an example that is particularly meaningful to you. This may be an example based on your personal experience or it may be one from the literature that sparked your interest or helped you see a gap in the field. To bring yourself into the text, be explicit about why and how your chosen example pertains to you. As you explain yourself, this might be one instance where you might want to use the first-person pronoun 'I'.[4] Later in this book, in Pointer 36, we consider a number of optional uses of the pronoun 'I'.

Another valuable consideration in your introductory chapter is how you situate yourself in your field of study. Situating yourself in the literature lets your reader get a sense of where the thesis is going and your place in it.

While a wide range of literature is presented in your literature review, your introductory chapter focuses on key literature that is important to you. This literature informs your reader of who you are as an academic and what you see as important. There are no sets of rules for how you introduce the literature in your introductory chapter. One possibility is to use your introductory chapter to cite those key authors who align with your thoughts, why you like their ideas, and what your research might add to their work. You can then use your literature review to elaborate on these key readings as well as a broader range of academic work in the field.

Another approach, if you have a strongly combative personality, is to introduce literature in your introductory chapter that presents an alternative positioning than yours,[5] and then highlight why this perspective (in your view) is inadequate (and who else agrees with you). If you start your thesis this way, your readers may expect you to maintain a combative positioning throughout the thesis.[6] This type of positioning requires a certain personality – someone who can both give and take criticism – because being heavily critical of others opens you up to similar forms of critique. Some of the critiques about your work might come from highly regarded people in the field (e.g., your examiners). If you can stand the heat, a combative approach might be for you. Researchers who use strong language tend to be cited (but unfortunately, not always in positive ways).

Another place where you can put yourself into your own writing in the introductory chapter is when you write the aims of your thesis. Many thesis writers tend to write the aims as very formal objective text. It doesn't have to be this way. You can think about explaining the aims of your thesis in ways that connect you to your reader. You might want to explain why you have certain research aims, and not others. You may want to use your description of your aims to introduce key terms and explain why they are of importance to you (further details about key terms are provided in Pointer 17).

The final part of your introduction is often your summary of what is to come, the overview of the thesis. The amount of content you provide here is an individual decision based on both how much detail you like to give to your audience and your stage in your degree. At the beginning stages of your thesis, you may have few details. It could be useful to leave this part of your thesis as an empty heading and think about writing this section of your introductory chapter as your thesis progresses. It is much easier to write about the content of the thesis when you have the requisite details to write the overview of each chapter with confidence.

Finally, remember that your introductory chapter will change as you finesse the content of your thesis. What you plan and what you do when you conduct your research can be very different. Also, what you see as important now may be very different after your research findings have been analyzed. An introductory chapter is often written and rewritten as your thesis progresses.

There are many guidebooks that provide useful tidbits about the content of your introductory chapter. Evans, Gruba and Justin (2011) manual is a good starting point. It provides useful tidbits on how to write a thesis. Kawase (2018) presents a quantitative examination of how others have structured their introductory chapter. The latter work provides you with various ways that you can structure an introductory chapter for an applied linguistics thesis, but the advice is useful to thesis writers in many different fields.

17. What's the big deal with definitions?

While thesis writers often work on bringing themselves into their introduction chapter, definitions can be particularly difficult to shape in ways you might want. This is because definitions necessarily involve concepts and ideas that have already been shaped by others.[7] To compose good definitions, you need to bring in the ideas of others as well as bring out your own. Well-crafted definitions set the groundwork for establishing your contribution to the field – your researcher identity – and how that identity relates to others in the field.

Definitions consist of two main parts. The key term and an explanation of what the key term means. A first important decision is whether you need a new key term. There may be an existing term that might work for you out there. If there is one, use it, and acknowledge where it came from. You don't want to create an entirely new term if it is not called for. The academic community will question why you need to create something different! If you believe your concept is sufficiently different so that the field requires a new key term, take time to carefully build up an argument that states clearly why a new term is needed.[8]

When you have decided on your key term, you next need to build your definition. This involves selectively choosing bits and pieces of information written by other academics in the field whose thinking aligns with yours, demonstrating how these bits reflect your identity as a researcher. Wording is always important, but it is especially the case in definitions. Every word

49

is subtly different from all others. To create a solid definition that meets your needs, think about all words in your definition (both separately and when combined), how each might be interpreted by others and, ultimately, what this might say about the way that *you* think.[9] Any change in wording (including the addition of something as small as 'a') offers up the potential to create a subtle shift in meaning to what is being defined. Just because some definitions are a sentence or two in length doesn't mean that they are easy to write.

Definitions are not complete without a surrounding text. Even when you believe that someone else has explained things in the ways that you intend, it is important to unpack your thinking. Have you considered all of the key parts of their definition and how each part is significant to you? Have you clarified any potential differences between your ideas and those of others, no matter how minor they may be. Take time to explain why certain words used in others' definitions are either inappropriate or less appropriate for your definition (see Pointer 32 on word choices in a thesis). By carefully explaining your thinking behind your key terms and their definitions, you simultaneously demonstrate your knowledge of the field, show how you align with a research community, and introduce the nuances you wish to convey. Strong definitions are hallmarks of a careful researcher.

Another crucial issue is consistency between one definition and another. As a researcher, you want a consistent voice. Your definitions are made up of elements that simultaneously distinguish and connect to each other. How are your definitions interconnected? Are there any ambiguities or contradictions? Carefully constructed definitions that link to one another are a strategic way of projecting an identity as someone knowledgeable about what they are writing and how that knowledge fits together.

There are other issues that you might like to consider, including how well your ways of knowing connect with your ways of doing. It is useful to keep a list of key terms and their definitions close (e.g., on a bulletin board in front of your computer) to ensure that your key terms are used consistently throughout your thesis in the ways that you have defined them. It is very easy to make changes in one part of your thesis and forget about how these changes affect later parts of your thesis.

Key terms and their definitions are important because they help your reader see your thinking process. This is one reason why definitions are introduced throughout the thesis. They can appear in your introductory chapter, literature review and methodology chapters of your thesis. Because of their importance, they are sometimes listed in the front matter.

For further reading on the difficulties with creating definitions, you might want to read Howe and Rancourt's (1990) work on how one emerging researcher struggled with defining terms in her doctoral thesis. You might also be interested in Stock and Burton's (2011) work on the importance of defining three commonly used terms in thesis writing: multi-disciplinary, inter-disciplinary and trans-disciplinary research, and the subtle differences between them.

18. Creating your research question

A research question drives your thesis, aiding you and your reader to stay on topic. How you word this question signals to the academic world the depth of your thinking about the topic as well as information about your theoretical and methodological positioning.

There are many things to consider. A very short research question can suggest that the thesis is broad in scope and lead some to consider that you haven't thought carefully enough about your topic. There are situations, however, where a short question can be quite useful. It works well if your thesis is exploratory in nature as it sends a message that the thesis and the thesis writer are open in their direction. A longer research question is much more informative to the reader; however, if not carefully worded, it can send the reader in multiple directions. For example, a research question with 'and' can suggest that the thesis aims to do two potentially different things.

Some research candidates think that a main question with a series of sub-questions is the answer, and it will be for some of you, as this gives structure to your thinking. Sub-questions give your reader the impression that you like to be thorough. But it may also suggest that you are not necessarily open to alternative thinking. In other words, there is no single answer as to how to structure your research question(s). You need to find a way that best represents you. Constructing research question(s) is not an easy task and you may be 'playing with' strings of words that forms your research question(s) for some time before you get it right.[10]

Another key consideration is the wording you choose in your research question. Words do not occur in isolation. They are embedded in the world and the words of those who use them. A research question full of general terms may give the impression that you are less knowledgeable about the field. In contrast, field-specific terms (if used appropriately) not only display an understanding of the field, but can even yell out to your reader your theoretical and methodological positioning. To give an example, 'language maintenance' was a key term in the 1980s for describing work helping minority communities to keep their minority language alive. There are hundreds (perhaps even thousands) of articles and books that have used this term. These days, the term *tends to be* found in papers that are more descriptive than theoretical, and it *tends to* appear in works that are not overly creative (e.g., replication studies). Such terms exist in all fields of research. Before you use any term in your research question, think carefully about any connotations it may have developed over its many years of use, and any identities that might be associated with it. If there is more than one key term in your research question, all terms need to be carefully considered together to ensure that they all are associated with the same theoretical positioning. Even mildly incompatible key terms in a research question can make you look like you don't know what you are doing.

While key terms in your research questions position you in the field, the verbs that you use in your research questions are also important as they can reflect the methodological thinking in your thesis and the direction that you want your thesis to take. They often indicate whether your thesis is an exploratory study, a descriptive study, a critique, a personal reflection, a theoretical debate etc. A thesis with a research question 'What aspects of supervision do supervisors *explore* in supervision sessions?' is a very different thesis than one which asks 'What aspects of supervision do supervisors *critique* in supervision sessions?' The choice of verb in your research question can influence the selection of key literature in your literature review, and even the methods employed in your methodology chapter.

Another key consideration is where to place the research question in your thesis. There are many possibilities. Some research candidates like to start the introduction with the research question. Others position it at the end of the introductory chapter – when they have established why such a question is justified. Still other thesis writers use their literature review to gradually build their research question. Some thesis writers like to remind their reader of their research question as they go through the thesis, while others think that this is too repetitive. While you do need to return to your research question towards the end of the thesis, as no thesis is complete without an answer to the question that drives it, all options are open as to where you first introduce your research question. As a first point of call, think about how you normally introduce a question in a conversation. How much information do you present before you ask a question? This might help you think about where your research question might be located.

For further reading, Agee (2009) provides a wealth of useful information about designing and structuring your research question.

19. Asserting yourself in your literature review

A literature review has two key functions. It captures and analyzes the relevant literature in your field of study and, equally importantly, it positions you within it. While you and your supervisor will focus on what literature is pertinent and valuable to your thesis topic, here we look at the ways that you can bring yourself into your literature review, something that can be challenging or even truly daunting at the beginning of your study. Early in your thesis journey you may feel that others have said it all, others have said it better, or that others are more knowledgeable or perhaps more senior and should be respected, rather than critiqued. Don't spend your valuable time worrying about this too much early on in your thesis journey. From the time you commence your thesis to the time you complete it, you will gain confidence, and become more knowledgeable and more nuanced in your claims.

While some of you may not start off confidently early in your thesis, avoid completely sabotaging your own voice in the meantime. There are some writing conventions that do just that. One strategy that prevents you from engaging with the literature is a general sentence followed by a list of parenthetical references (e.g., 'Various researchers have discussed this issue (references 1,2,3)'. When you employ parenthetical references, it makes it difficult for you to unpack what you have read, what these authors have to say, and how you feel about their research.[11]

A relatively easy way of starting to bring yourself into the literature review is to adjust your sentence structure to make the authors of your cited works the subject of your sentences. This sentence structure necessarily requires a reporting verb, e.g., Starks and Robertson (2022) 'introduce, mention, describe, summarize, expand on, evaluate, or critique' a particular point. The careful selection of the right verb not only shows that you have read the literature carefully, but also positions you to get out of the back seat and engage with the various authors that have made substantial contributions in your area of study. A carefully selected verb can change your text from a dry chronological representation of the literature to a lucid analysis of how researchers have contributed to the literature in ways that connect with your thinking. Drafting sentences in this way changes the text from one that reports or summarizes to one that analyzes what others have written.

Strategically placed adjectives present you with further opportunities to characterize how you feel about ideas (e.g., Starks and Robertson (2022) introduce 'innovative ideas' or perhaps 'noteworthy points'). The use of well-placed adjectives provides a way to bring yourself into your literature review and can help you build confidence about your contribution to knowledge, and the ways that you wish to position your own research with it. We return to how various types of verbs and adjectives can be used to enhance your writing in Chapter 5.

After you have completed each section in your literature review, you might find it useful to end each section with a simple summary statement about gaps that remain to be filled, which gaps you aim to fill (or at least build on), and your reasons for doing this. Gaps-in-the-field sentences bring you into the centre of your analysis of the literature. They have one additional advantage. These sentences provide supervisor(s) with useful points of discussion and provide you with opportunities to defend your positioning in ways that strengthen your arguments. Discussions with your supervisor(s) about what you see as research gaps can be particularly useful in the initial stages of your literature review when your supervisor(s) is/are still learning to understand how you think.

For further reading, both Pautasso (2013) and Webster and Watson (2002) write about the importance of bringing yourself into the literature review in two fields of study. Ridley (2012) provides general details about the importance of introducing your own voice into your literature review in Chapter 9 of *Literature review: A step-by-step guide for students*. Chang and Schleppegrell (2011) focus on how lexical choices can be used to develop an argument that allows you to position the literature and create a niche for your own work. For an in-depth analysis of the process of writing a literature review, we recommend Efron and Ravid (2019). For a detailed analysis of the typical component parts of a literature review, Ridley (2012) is a useful resource. For how the literature review can be organized, you might like a read of Randolph (2009).

20. How you can write up your research methodology

Supervisors often tell thesis writers that the methodology chapter needs to include a detailed description of how the research was completed. There are many guidebooks to inform you about which details to include (e.g., descriptions of the research site, the research question, the methods used to collect the data, ways to analyze the data, ethical concerns etc. [e.g., Carey, 2009]). You can also obtain a range of useful ideas about the requisite parts of a methodology chapter from reading other theses.

The writings of researchers who use similar methodologies to you are also useful. Although their research question and even the topic may differ greatly from your thesis, the works cover similar methodological underpinnings. Through close reading, you can learn to emulate a particular way of thinking and writing that makes you sound like the researcher you want to be.

Another issue you might think about is the text type that you use to give structure to your methodology chapter. When you start to write your methodology chapter, there are different text types that you can choose. Finding a text type that fits with your identity as a thesis writer can keep you focused and motivated and give you greater control over your writing. This is because each text type has a very different 'feel'. If you are the kind of person who likes to focus on how things come together, you might organize your methodology chapter as a descriptive text with each section outlining the requisite parts of your research design and how each is necessary (or at least useful) for answering your research question. As an example, you could write a description of your research site (within the limits permitted by your ethical approval) and in that description explain how this location is a suitable, logical or even the best location to allow you to answer your research question. You then use the same type of text structure to describe your research participants.

Alternatively, if you are someone who likes to tell stories and your supervisors are amenable to you writing your methodology chapter (or the entire thesis) in this way, you might want to consider writing your methodology chapter as a carefully constructed story of why you set about to conduct this study, the setting in which the story took place, the events that unfolded (the findings of the case study, the survey results etc.), and how these relate back to the purpose of your journey (i.e., its implications). Throughout your story you can provide evaluative commentary about any issues that emerged along the way and how they were resolved. A story has the added advantage of making your text come alive, and it is the best text type if you want your reader to remember all that you have written. Once you have heard a good story, the details are rarely forgotten.[12]

Another approach is to organize your methodology chapter as a procedural text where you first introduce the requisite parts (e.g., the research setting, the participants, interview schedule, coding etc.) and then describe the procedures you adopted. As with all text types, as you write you need to explain each part of your research design and justify how it helps to answer your research question. You may find procedural text types useful if you are conducting a quantitative study or if you are keen for future researchers to replicate your study, but you could also use it for any thesis type.

There are still other ways to construct your methodology chapter. As we suggested in Chapter 2, it may be possible for you to design your chapter around a cultural metaphor, outlining how each part of your cultural metaphor relates back to each decision made about how you conducted your research, why you conducted your research in that way, and how this relates to your research question.

As you are writing your methodology chapter, there is one additional issue that every thesis writer asks. How much detail is needed? This is a crucial question as too much detail may result in the loss of the grand narrative/argument; too little, and there may not be enough details for others to replicate your study and give it rigor. You can arrive at some ideas about whether you tend to write too much or too little by looking at how you interact with others. Some people don't explain enough in their daily life, others give too much detail.

Deciding how much detail to provide in your methodology chapter can still be difficult as relevance can be hard to determine. Do you need to mention the position of the chair you were sitting in when you conducted interviews, and whether you weren't feeling well on the day? If the answers had some effect on the quality of the data produced, then the answer might be 'yes'. But the answer could also be 'not really' if this information is not pertinent to your research question. In many instances, you mightn't know what to include or exclude until you have analyzed your data and you have thought about how your methods have informed your findings. This unknowing is partly what makes a methodology chapter so difficult to write, and why a methodology chapter is often written and rewritten. As a rule of thumb, the more thorough you are, the more likely your reader will be able to replicate your study (if ever you become famous!). As you will always fail to mention something that others think is relevant, it is important to explain why you are giving the details that you give. It may also be useful to explain why you think it is unimportant to focus on certain details. A reader (or examiner) won't complain too strongly about what you have done if they can see your reasons, especially if these relate to your overall methodological positioning.

To understand the importance of placing yourself in the writing world, there are other sources that you might find useful. You might like to read St. Pierre's (2018) description of her doctoral research journey and the need to write methodology in ways that demonstrate a thorough understanding of the theoretical perspective that you are using in your work.

21. Writing up your findings and discussion?

How-to guides to thesis writing provide a list of valuable components to include when writing up your findings and discussing the relevance and importance of your research (see for example, Ryan, 2006). However, there is another important component of the writing process –incorporating you.

As a thesis writer, there are different ways that you can organize this part of your thesis. If you can envisage two or more ways that you can structure your data and its analysis, you might consider the various choices and ultimately go with what you consider to be the best fit for the data you have available to you. If, for example, your thesis centres on the need to redefine concepts in the field, you could dedicate one chapter to the ways that definitions and terms need to be developed and a following chapter to explain how these new definitions help create new ways of seeing the world. The overriding aim of your thesis should be to get it written, using any approach that helps your thesis progress. As long as you carefully explain your ways of doing, everything is possible. This is partly why it is hard to write up your findings. There are many options available.

Another decision to make is how many chapters do you need and how do you organize them. There is no set number of chapters that a thesis must have. If you are a person who likes to put things into neat boxes, you may find separating your thoughts into multiple chapters useful (as long as you don't separate out your bits so much that you lose track of the underlying story). Separating ideas out into different chapters can be particularly beneficial if you have multiple forms of data to present, and multiple variables that need to be analyzed. Depending on your data, you may want separate chapters to consider different research questions. You might also like to have separate chapters that consider different participant perspectives, especially if they provide complementary or conflicting answers to any of your research questions.

Another consideration is whether you separate your findings from your discussion. Some of you may find it more to your liking to integrate the findings and discussion. This can useful if you want to interpret, question and evaluate as you go. If you take this approach, you are likely to cover fewer of your findings but cover those findings in greater depth.

In other words, the choices that you make reflect both you, the data you have, and how you feel about the most powerful way of presenting that data. Take time to play around with all these points to investigate how the mega-narrative of your thesis is best represented.

For further reading, you could look at Makar et al. (2018). They present a series of very useful points about how to structure the content of a discussion chapter. While this work provides insights into structuring the thesis, you should note that some language features that they recommend are ones that distance you from your writing (i.e., passive sentences).

22. What's your conclusion?

Although there are works that include information about what should be in a concluding chapter of a thesis (e.g., González-López & López López, 2020), there are relatively few that talk about how your concluding chapter serves as a reflection of you. So, how do you wrap up your work in ways that let you bring yourself into the text?

The way you construct your concluding chapters says a lot about what you see as important. Are you someone who likes to emphasize the main points and emphasize their importance, or are you someone who would be more likely to focus on their limitations? A key consideration is how you wish others to think about you, as a researcher. Are you someone who wants to use the concluding chapter to focus on the limitations of your work and how things could be improved, or someone who wants to use the concluding chapter to focus on the significance of your work in the grander scheme of things, with any mention of potential improvements treated as subordinate to your main point. Where you place your focus is up to you, but most people want to show themselves and their thesis in the best light possible. That doesn't mean ignoring limitations; it just means not making a big deal about them.

There are still other considerations. Do you see the concluding chapter as the central place for introducing other future projects, or do you feel that you should keep these tidbits neatly tucked away so that you can use them another day?

Another consideration is how to place your emphasis on connecting back to work in the field. You could choose to be backward looking, focusing on what you have done but you could also choose to be forward looking, using your concluding chapter as an opportunity to explore the potential significance of your work for other projects. You could focus on how the thesis sets the stage for your later work, including a list of your next endeavors. This approach could have positive repercussions. It might even encourage like-minded souls working in similar areas to approach you for collaborative research.

Still another possibility is to place yourself firmly at the centre of the concluding chapter. How did you find the thesis writing experience? The concluding chapter might focus on what you found to be the most difficult/rewarding? While thesis writers often write something about each of the above points, the amount you write, and the sequencing of them, reflects the relative importance of these issues for you.

With so many options, it's unfortunate that many thesis writers leave this chapter too late. Concluding chapters written towards the end of candidature tend to be written under duress. Time limits and the sheer exhaustion associated with reaching the final stages can make you forget about yourself as a writer and incline you to simply want to finish the thesis. There are many advantages of drafting bits of your concluding chapter early on. Writing the concluding chapter part way through your findings may give a greater sense that you are able to finish your thesis. It may also allow you to focus on what you have to say and its contribution to the academic world. For further information about writing thesis conclusions, you might like to consider Evans et al. (2011), who provide insights into how to write conclusions to chapters, and conclusions to the thesis as a whole.

23. Which referencing style is for you?

There are so many referencing styles, which begs the question: which one should you use? Some universities prescribe specific styles; disciplines sometimes sway thesis writers to use a referencing style. Using the preferred referencing style of the discipline can be useful: it makes you look like you are on the same team (a researcher in a particular discipline). Yet when writing a multi-, inter- or trans-disciplinary work, choosing an appropriate referencing style can be tricky. If you publish parts of your thesis by/with publication. you may be confronted with varied referencing styles, (see Pointer 24 for further details).

While the differences in referencing conventions may seem rather arbitrary, there is some logic involved. Some differences reflect the relative importance that the field places on certain types of information. We illustrate this point with examples. The preferred style for many humanities disciplines is MLA; the guide published by the Modern Language Association. In this referencing style, in the reference list, the given names of authors are presented in full rather than presented as initials. When referring to an author of a novel, the standard convention in the field of humanities is that you refer to the authors by their full name (don't ask us why, we don't know!). Even if you are not in the humanities, you are aware of this convention. You may know the full names of many well-known authors (e.g., Shakespeare's first name was William, and Austin's first name was Jane). The use of full given names reflects a standard convention in the field. A second referencing convention in MLA relates to the date of publication. The date of publication in the MLA referencing style guide dictates that it is to be located at the very end of each entry in your reference list. This information is presented last because it makes no difference to the quality or relevance of the work when a play or novel was published. The importance of people over dates is also reflected in-text citations, but a bit more subtly. When citing multiple in-text references using MLA referencing conventions, authors are ordered according to the surname of the authors (Robertson, 2020; Starks, 2021).

When writing in the social sciences, a preferred referencing style is APA; the guide published by the American Psychological Association. Here, the given name of the author has less importance, and any author's first name is reduced to initials. This lack of interest in given names is reflected elsewhere in the field. When you refer to authors in seminars in the social sciences, you typically refer to them by their surname only. In an APA reference list, the date of publication follows the name of the author because the date of publication has more significance in social sciences. The findings of a study published in 1960 are typically not considered as relevant as those published in 2022.

Another common style manual is the Chicago Manual of Style. It is used by many fields of study, including history. This is a particularly useful style guide when authors need to acknowledge that a narrative, and even an epistemological positioning is contestable. Here, because the nature of the source of knowledge matters, complete bibliographical information is presented as footnotes on the page where the content is being discussed. In this referencing style, the text need not contain a bibliography,[13] as all references are listed in their order of appearance in the text.

If those aren't enough options for you, at regular intervals, new versions of style guides appear that reflect changing conditions. As an example, in APA7, the place of publication of books is no longer required in reference lists. This makes sense because books are increasingly published online, and hard copies are published in multiple locations. Newer editions of style guides also include details about new types of publications. The seventh edition of the style APA guide, for example, contains ways to reference a greater selection of electronic works than earlier editions.

In some instances, you may be told that *any* referencing style is acceptable. The only condition is that your referencing style should be consistent. This is more difficult than it sounds. If you cut and paste references from different sources or try to convert a list of references from one referencing style to another, you may find yourself being inconsistent. Referencing programs such as EndNote or Bib TeX can help you to maintain consistency. These programs enable you to change all references from one style to another at the click of a single button, altering all punctuation and capitalization that differs from one style to the next.[14] You nonetheless need to check your references. Sometimes when citations are downloaded, they can appear without journal page numbers and with inaccurate punctuation. The referencing programs don't add missing information. You have to do this yourself.

There is a little more to consider. When you are writing your thesis by/with publication, you may notice that sometimes a publisher has a style guide that is only 'sort of' APA. British publishers often request manuscripts follow British spelling and punctuation conventions to make their works read more British-like. Other times, publishers may request APA, but ask you to provide the full given names of every author in any reference list so that readers can more readily search to locate authors, and their works. It is much easier to search for an author or editor if you know their full name. It's crucial to read publishing guidelines carefully so you know how each publisher wants you to reference.

Whatever the style that you use, supervisors and examiners share a common expectation. They expect you to be very thorough in documenting all details of all references and that these details are formatted using an appropriate referencing style. If you are not a very tidy researcher or you are short on time, you might want to pay an editor to check your references before you submit your thesis.

24. Is a thesis by/with publication for you?

Instead of a traditional thesis (a monograph), many universities are now offering research candidates a wealth of alternatives (Anderson & Okuda, 2021; Honan & Bright, 2016). In some disciplines, this may involve an artistic performance (see Hunter, 2009), and in disciplines that focus on construction or design, it may involve the demonstration of some sort of practice (Yee, 2010). Your thesis may be presented as a media production (e.g., a documentary). These days, a thesis can even be constructed as a dialogue (Weatherall, 2019).

While options are increasingly open, one that attracts many research candidates is a thesis by/with publication. This option is an inviting one for some thesis writers, but it may not be for all. If you need to finish your thesis quickly, you may find a thesis by/with publication impractical, as publishing typically involves a lot more work.

Thesis writers who are challenged when members of their supervisory team provide what seems to be contradictory comments can likewise find a thesis by/with publication difficult. Even though supervisor(s) can sometimes provide differing feedback, your supervisor(s) know what you want to achieve in your overall thesis, and you can be relatively confident that they are working towards this common goal. The multiple reviewers of your intended publications are not invested in, nor do they have knowledge of, your work as a whole. For an effective thesis by/with publication, it is important to see the overall story early in your thesis journey so that you are acutely aware when reviewers make suggestions about publications that can change your overall thesis narrative. This may mean that you sometimes need to argue against reviewers who are advocating changes that conflict with that thesis storyline (or your supervisors' storyline if you are funded by a grant). It takes courage to argue with the reviewer/editor and to risk losing a publication because required revisions don't fit your overall thesis. It is here where your supervisory team is essential as they have the experience needed to direct you in this task.

A thesis writer who writes a thesis by/with publications needs to be willing to conceive of a thesis as if it is a collective enterprise. Any publications, whether co-authored or not, involve more from the supervisory team than if you were to complete a traditional thesis. There needs to be frank discussions throughout the thesis journey about everyone's role during and post-graduation as there is a high likelihood of outstanding publications which will need to be finalized well after the thesis is submitted. You need to be confident that you can work as a team for the duration, potentially years after you have graduated. To keep your supervisors with you during this long haul, you may need to think about co-publishing your work.

As a thesis by/with publication is a collective work, you need to talk through all reviewer comments with your supervisor(s) as even minor changes may not align with the wording and arguments of other publications (by you and potentially by other members of the research team). Important areas where you need to pay careful attention are key terms and their definitions (refer to Pointer 17 for further details) as any change in key terms will not fare well when you put the thesis together as a whole. If key terms have been pre-established by your supervisory team (or other members of your group), you will need to use them consistently across any and all publications related to the project. Key terms may be revised, but any revisions need to be fully acknowledged in publications.[15]

Other points to consider before embarking on a thesis by/with publication relate to your ability to write to a strict word limit. Thesis writers who like to be precise and stay focused on one topic can find thesis by/with publication easier than those who like to elaborate extensively on what they write because publications have strict word limits. As you go through the publication process, reviewers typically ask for more details and many editors, nonetheless, ask that you keep to their word limits. It is not an easy task to cut 2,000 or even 200 words out of a highly crafted submitted manuscript that has already undergone extensive editing. In most cases, though, further editing is well worth it, as it often greatly improves the final text. The supervisory team is important here as different individuals see different ways of editing down the word count of a text.

An obvious difference between a traditional thesis and a thesis by/with publication is authorship. Any thesis by/with publication is likely to have a complex set of authorships. You may have a single authorship in one publication, and co-authorships of various types in other works. It is crucial to establish early on how the lead author will be established, as well as the order of all authors in any co-publication. Being comfortable with your supervisory team is a priority, as is trust. A good understanding of who will be doing what, and a willingness to be flexible and adjust to fluid circumstances in the publication game, are important.

It may not always be easy to work together, as members of your supervisory team have different agendas. A quick publication in a local research journal will not increase your supervisors' reputations and your supervisors may not want to co-author any such publication. Stronger publications have other issues. They typically go through multiple reviews and rewrites and these publications may not be ready within the time for your candidature. These and other issues need to be considered early in your thesis candidature so that everyone is on the same page. Other discussions could include whether it would be useful to write a short commentary in a local journal about the aims and value of the proposed project. If a collective grant funds your project, this may need to be a collective publication; if your project is unfunded, you may have more opportunities for you to have a quick single-authored publication. You may also want to talk amongst your supervision team how one publication can act as a prelude to the next (e.g., whether it would be useful to write a paper on data collection prior to writing about the findings). Discussing these options early and being sensitive to potential tensions involved will help to avoid issues later.

A final issue that you may want to consider before embarking on a thesis by/with publication is coherence. Are you someone who is willing to accept a little incoherence? Publications often don't fit together well. While pronouns cause no issues in each individual publication, they can make your overall thesis slightly incoherent if 'I' refers to the author in some publications, and 'we' in others. Another key difference in co-authored works is voice. If your research supervisor co-authors a paper with you, do you write the first draft (to give a singular voice to the manuscript) or do you each write separate parts and edit it later for a singular voice? Or do you accept that the paper may differ in its voice? In other words, can you accept a thesis with slight differences in writing styles in different parts of a thesis by/with publication?

Even when writing a thesis by/with publication as a sole author, journal requirements will mean that your thesis is full of incoherence. Each journal has its own requirements. Differences can include the length and structure of abstracts, heading types, formatting (in-text references and bibliography), and overall word length. Word limits can range substantially, meaning some chapters will be much shorter than others. If these issues bother you, you may want to stick with a traditional thesis, and publish an article or two on the side. However, if you thrive as a member of a team, minor coherence issues don't irk you, and you can handle the extra publication pressures, then the thesis by/with publication route may be for you.

For further reading on the thesis by/with publication option, check out Merga et al. (2020) on the pros and cons of writing an Australian thesis by publication. For additional insights, Mason and Merga (2018) provide a useful summary of different macro-structures that research candidates have used to integrate their publications into a thesis format. Lindqvist (2018) provides an interesting case study of the review process of articles submitted for publication as part of a four-year doctoral study in a European setting and Matteson and DeLozier (2022) provide insights into this genre in an American institution.

Notes

1   A thesis by/with publication is typically a series of publications bound together by an introductory and concluding chapter. A thesis with publication(s) is typically a thesis that includes one or more publications. The 'with publication' option tends to include a higher proportion of unpublished work. Every university has their own rules around what you can submit as a publication. It's important to read the guidelines carefully.

2   Using an example as part of your title helps your readers remember your work, but it can also hinder others from finding it. If your title doesn't contain key words, computer searches may overlook your thesis.

3   If you are someone who thinks a story is not the best way to begin a thesis, you still might write a story about what motivated you to complete your thesis. You can pin it to your bulletin board to inspire you on days when you are thinking the thesis is all too hard.

4   Check with your supervisors early on about how you want to write and what they might expect. It may be useful to start the discussion with a piece of writing, with notes in the comment box such as 'I used the pronoun 'I' here because I wanted to emphasize the point'. This use of comments differentiates issues about writing from those about thesis content.

5   All academics have personal as well as academic identities. While it is okay to be personal and passionate, academic identities tend to be measured because there is always something 'right' in every positioning.

6   While a polarized stance may not be for everyone, there is no harm in writing this way 'for your eyes only'. It might help you to crystalize your argument. It can also help you to vent some steam.

7   We would like to thank Howard Nicholas for his insightful commentary on an earlier version of this book. He raised the point about the need to consider the duality of voices when constructing definitions that helped reshape this Pointer.

8   If you feel the need for a new key word, it may be useful to create a term that bears a similarity to a related term in the literature. This provides an opportunity to highlight the differences between your term and that of others.

9   Examiners pay a lot of attention to the wording of your definitions. If the wording is ambiguous, unclear, or perhaps too broad or too restrictive, it enables them to critique underlying assumptions in your work.

10   Research questions might change a little once you have collected your data. Be prepared to refine your research question at every key part of your thesis journey.

11   Parenthetical referencing can be useful when you want to show familiarity with a broad range of literature on a topic. Parenthetical referencing has a good ground-clearing role as it permits you to demonstrate that you are aware of more than you can discuss in detail in your thesis. The materials may be related to the topic but have little relevance to your main argument. Parenthetical referencing has some of the same functions as a footnote.

12   Some cultural traditions place the onus of drawing a conclusion on the audience. A thesis ending written in academic English needs to be explicit in its conclusions. When writing your conclusion, think as if you are explaining the point of your story to someone who may not have been listening very carefully.

13   There are two versions of the Chicago referencing style, one that uses footnotes for bibliographical entries and one that uses both footnotes and a final reference list.

14   Programs such as Endnote save you endless hours reformatting your references from one referencing style to another when you publish a chapter of your thesis in a journal. They also save you time if that journal rejects your manuscript and you need to resubmit to another journal with a different stylesheet.

15   If you want to downplay an issue, acknowledging any change in the use of a key term in a footnote. If you want to highlight the change, explore it in your main text.

References

Abdel Salam El-Dakhs, Dina. (2018). Why are abstracts in PhD theses and research articles different? A genre-specific perspective. *Journal of English for Academic Purposes, 36*, 48–60. https://doi.org/10.1016/j.jeap.2018.09.005

Agee, Jane. (2009). Developing qualitative research questions: A reflective process. *International Journal of Qualitative Studies in Education, 22*(4), 431–447. https://doi.org/10.1080/09518390902736512

Anderson, Tim, & Okuda, Tomoyo (2021). Temporal change in dissertation macro-structures. *English for Specific Purposes, 64,* 1–12. https://doi.org/10.1016/j.esp.2021.06.001

Carey, Malcolm. (2009). *The social work dissertation: Using small-scale qualitative methodology.* Open University Press.

Chang, Peicin, & Schleppegrell, Mary. (2011). Taking an effective authorial stance in academic writing: Making the linguistic resources explicit for L2 writers in the social sciences. *English for Academic Purposes, 10,* 140–151. http://dx.doi.org/10.1016/j.jeap.2011.05.005

Efron, Sara Efrat, & Ravid, Ruth. 2019. *Writing the literature review: A practical guide.* The Guilford Press.

Evans, David, et al. (2011). *How to write a better thesis.* (3rd ed.). Springer. https://doi.org/10.1007/978-3-319-04286-2_6

Galvan, Jose L., & Galvan, Melisa C. (2017). *Writing literature reviews: A guide for students of the social and behavioral sciences.* (7th ed.). Routledge. https://doi.org/10.4324/9781315229386

Goffman, Erving. (1959, reprinted 2022). *Presentation of self in everyday life.* Penguin.

González-López, Samuel, & Aurelio López López. (2020). Assessing thesis conclusions by their connectedness with goal, judgment and speculation. *Revista Signos-Estudios de Lingüística, 53*(104), 643–663. https://doi.org/10.4067/S0718-09342020000300643

Honan, Eileen, & Bright, David. (2016). Writing a thesis differently. *International Journal of Qualitative studies in Education, 29*(5), 731–743. https://doi.org/10.1080/09518398.2016.1145280

Howe, Christine, & Rancourt, Ann M. (1990). The importance of definitions of selected concepts for leisure inquiry. *Leisure Sciences, 12*(4), 395–406. https://doi.org/10.1080/01490409009513117

Hunter, Victoria Margaret. (2009). Site-specific dance performance: The investigation of a creative process. University of Leeds.

Hyland, Ken. (2004). Graduates' gratitude: The generic structure of dissertation acknowledgements. *English for Specific Purposes, 23*(4), 303–324. https://doi.org/10.1016/s0889-4906(03)00051-6

Kaplan, Robert B., et al. (1994). On abstract writing. *Text-Interdisciplinary Journal for the study of discourse, 14*(3), 401–426. https://doi.org/10.1515/text.1.1994.14.3.401

Kawase, Tomoyuki. (2018). Rhetorical structure of the introductions of applied linguistics PhD theses. *Journal of English for Academic Purposes, 31,* 18–27. https://doi.org/10.1016/j.jeap.2017.12.005

Kumar, Vijay, & Sanderson, Lara J. (2020). The effects of acknowledgements in doctoral theses on examiners. *Innovations in Education and Teaching International, 57*(3), 285–295. https://doi.org/10.1080/14703297.2019.1620625

Lindqvist, Marcia Håkansson. (2018) Reconstructing the doctoral publishing process. Exploring the liminal space. *Higher Education Research & Development*, *37*(7), 1395–1408. https://doi.org/10.1080/07294360.2018.1483323

Makar, Gabriel, et al. (2018). How to write effective discussion and conclusion sections. *Clinical Spine Surgery*, *31*(8), 345–346. https://doi.org/10.1097/BSD.0000000000000687

Mason, Shannon, & Merga, Margaret. (2018). Integrating publications in the social science doctoral thesis by publication. *Higher Education Research and Development*, *37*(7), 1454–1471. https://doi.org/10.1080/07294360.2018.1498461

Matteson, Shirley Marie, & DeLozier, Rebecca W. (2022). Undertaking a three-article dissertation. In Aaron Samuel Zimmerman (Ed.), *Methodological innovations in research and academic writing* (pp. 240–259). IGI Global. https://doi.org/10.4018/978-1-7998-8283-1

Merga, Margaret K, et al. (2020). 'What do I even call this?' Challenges and possibilities of undertaking a thesis by publication. *Journal of Further and Higher Education*, *44*(9), 1245–1261. https://doi.org/10.1080/0309877X.2019.1671964

Morton, Janne, & Storch, Neomy. (2019). Developing an authorial voice in PhD multilingual student writing: The reader's perspective. *Journal of Second Language Writing*, *49*, 15–23. https://doi.org/10.1016/j.jslw.2018.02.0

Pautasso, Marco. (2013). Ten simple rules for writing a literature review. *PLOS Computational Biology*. https://journals.plos.org/ploscompbiol/article?id=10.1371/journal.pcbi.1003149

Randolph, Justus. (2009) A guide to writing the dissertation literature review. *Practical Assessment, Research and Evaluation*, *14*(13). https://doi.org/10.7275/b0az-8t74

Ridley, Diana. (2012). *Literature review: A step-by-step guide for students*. (2nd ed.). SAGE.

Ryan, Anne B. (2006). Analysing qualitative data and writing up your findings. In Mary Antonesa (Ed.), *Researching and writing your thesis: A guide for postgraduate students* (pp. 92–108). Maynooth Adult and Community Education.

St. Pierre, Elizabeth Adams. (2018). Writing post-qualitative inquiry. *Qualitative Inquiry*, *24*(9), 603–608. https://doi.org/10.1177%2F1077800417734567

Stock, Paul, & Burton, Rob J. F. (2011). Defining terms for integrated (multi-inter-trans-disciplinary) sustainability research. *Sustainability*, *3*, 1090–1113. https://doi.org/10.3390/su3081090

Weatherall, Ruth. (2019). Writing the doctoral thesis differently. *Management Learning*, *50*(1), 100–113. https://doi.org/10.1177/1350507618799867

Webster, Jane, & Watson, Richard T. (2002). Analyzing the past to prepare for the future: Writing a literature review. *Management Information Systems Quarterly*, *26*(2), 8–12. https://www.jstor.org/stable/4132319

Yee, Joyce S. R. (2010). Methodological innovation in practice-based design doctorates. *Journal of Research Practice*, *6*(2), Article M15. http://jrp.icaap.org/index.php/jrp/article/view/196/193

Writing yourself into your thesis in small but important ways

5

Overview

Readers react to classic advice on thesis writing in guidebooks in different ways. Some readers find the advice useful, others find it somewhat daunting and difficult to reconcile with their own writer identity. Sometimes it is a bit of both, without really understanding why this is so. In every piece of writing, there is always more than one way to argue a point, more than one way to present your text, and more than one way to bring yourself into it. The pointers in Chapter 5 are centered around writing academic text and how to make your ideas and words stand out so that they make an impact. In other words, it's about the normally boring procedural stuff and ways that you can make it work for you.

In this chapter, we introduce 14 pointers that engage with parts of language that enable your text to cohere while keeping your identity central to your thesis. These include pointers around headings, paragraph and sentence structures as well as hints about using footnotes and appendices so that you can tuck away information to make your text flow. We consider tenses you might use to write your thesis (or parts thereof), and information about word types that might help you fine-tune textual clarity. The chapter explores pronoun choices associated with authorship. These include how you might like to use the pronoun 'I' and pronouns (and other devices) that you might like to use to refer to your cited authors. The chapter ends with comments about differences in the ways that individuals use the English language and why this isn't something that you need to dwell on when writing your thesis. As many editing decisions are individual ones, our intent is that you take our suggestions and use them in ways that fit you and norms in

DOI: 10.4324/9781003323402-5

the field with which you identify. Feel free to ignore any ideas entirely if they don't fit with your own thesis writer identity.

Figure 5.1 Small changes can make big differences

25. Your headings

Perhaps the easiest way to organize ideas is through headings. Headings are used to guide readers to the main points of your text.[1] Well-designed headings provide readers (including your supervisor(s)) with strong clues as to how to read your thesis the way that you want it to be read.

There is a lot of flexibility in the ways that you can compose headings. They can be generic, serving simply to separate out main ideas (e.g., Participants, Methods, Ethics). They can be more personalized and specific (e.g., 'My journey', 'My purpose', 'My starting ideas' or 'My problem'), providing greater insights into the intended purposes of the text that follows. As an example, the introductory chapter of Margaret Robertson's thesis was titled 'The Map' to give her readers a sense that the themes of her research are best perceived as a journey to be explored throughout the thesis. In some instances, headings provide insights into your approach. As examples of the latter, your methods might be worded as 'The reasons for using a qualitative approach for my study'; or the description of your participants labeled as 'The type of people vital for my study'.[2]

There is lots of choice around how many headings you use. Some of you may prefer to use many headings, others a few, and still others, none at all.

Those of you who use headings extensively might like to number them. This lets you keep track of the number of points made, their order and the subparts therein. For others of you, numbered headings make your hair stand up. They are far too formal. If you use lots of headings, but you don't like to use numbering to organize them, you may like to try organizing your headings and subheadings through various types of fonts and indentation.

While it is important to think about the structure and wording of headings, it is also important to think about how they serve different purposes at varying stages of your thesis. In initial drafts, they can be useful for editing. Headings segment text into parts, making it easier to locate sections of text, move sections of text (or parts thereof) from one place to another and make decisions about what to cut out. They save you slaving through every sentence when the point you originally wanted to make in a section of your thesis is no longer relevant.

As your thesis is always in a state of development, headings shouldn't be seen as final but rather seen as scaffolding to be modified as work progresses. When you have completed your thesis, if you are certain that you have covered the topic and presented the main points in the best possible order, you might decide to keep all headings in your final draft or delete some to create more emphasis on the macro-structures.

Remember to check the wording of your headings on a regular basis to ensure that they are a true reflection of the content that follows. During your thesis, some ideas will disappear, others will change and re-emerge in different configurations.

26. What about paragraph length?

Paragraphs are another way of structuring your text. While paragraphs naturally vary in length depending on what you want to say about a particular topic, by-and-large, each writer tends to have their own pattern. Just open a few random books on your bookshelf to observe differences. Some people write paragraphs that have very complex structures, with multiple strands; others like to segment their paragraphs into succinct units.

To write effectively, it's useful to understand a few things about paragraph length. We will start with the long paragraphs, but for no particular reason. Some thesis writers can write successful long paragraphs; however, many thesis writers who tend to write sequences of complex ideas in paragraphs of half a page or more run into difficulty. Readers often find sequences of complex thoughts difficult to unpack. If parts of your paragraphs happen to be somewhat untidy (e.g., containing thoughts that have not been explained in detail), long paragraphs can become incomprehensible. If your supervisor remarks that some of your ideas are not clear, you could find it useful to shorten those paragraphs to divide your thoughts into smaller units. Shorter paragraphs help you stay on point and help your supervisor and examiners understand what you have to say.

This next paragraph is written for those of you who like to be direct and to the point. Although some of your paragraphs may work perfectly well, others may not always contain enough information for your reader to follow all of what you want to say. You might want to think about what each of your sentences in your paragraph is doing. Do you have a topic sentence that states what the paragraph is about or explains its importance for your readership? Do you provide any commentary on how other authors think about the topic discussed in the paragraph? Do you give an example to illustrate your point? If any of these questions point to potential holes in your paragraphs, you should consider expanding your paragraphs a little to add more clarity to what you are trying to say. Remember, though, not all paragraphs need to include all the above points.

To write for impact, it is useful to think about changing it up a little every now and then. If you consistently write longish paragraphs, a short paragraph draws your reader's attention to the text and what is written therein. If you consistently write short paragraphs, an extra-long paragraph has a similar effect. It signals that the point raised in this paragraph is more complicated, requires more attention, or is even more significant than other paragraphs in that section of the thesis.

As you play around with your optimal paragraph lengths, you might want to think about writing short paragraph structures in initial drafts, for when you have incomplete thoughts. These can signal that a thought needs to be developed. You could supplement this short paragraph with a note in the margin to say to your supervisory team that you need to expand on this idea and what might be preventing you from doing so. Short paragraphs can lead some supervisors to suggest ideas about potential subject matter for that paragraph.

27. What is so important about topic sentences?

Another way that you can bring yourself into your writing is through the ways that you start each paragraph. Many guidebooks recommend the use of topic sentences as they provide guidance to the reader about the purpose of the paragraph, and sometimes they also provide an indication of its key ideas. While topic sentences are often considered a key feature for academic writing, they can be troublesome for those of you who like to structure ideas in different ways, due to cultural background, prior education and even personal preference. Topic sentences can make you feel that you are giving away too much information too early. They can even make your text sound awfully rigid if your heart is not into them. If you don't like topic sentences, but your supervisor(s) is/are asking you to write them all the same, you might want to write your topic sentences after you have completed your paragraphs (see summary sentences in Pointer 28). Another possibility is to write your thesis in ways that don't require many topic sentences. If you compose your thesis as a story, you won't need as many topic sentences as good stories contain paragraphs that don't aim to spoil the suspense of what comes next. They rarely contain topic sentences.

While topic sentences are useful in the final version of your thesis, they have additional uses at various stages of the thesis-writing journey. They are convenient ways of ensuring your initial text stays on track. If you are someone who likes to write and think at the same time, you may start to write a paragraph with one thought but end up with a slightly different one. In that case, a quick recheck with your topic sentence after your paragraph is complete will determine if your initial topic sentence guides the reader to the actual content of the paragraph.

You may also find topic sentences a great way to polish your text. If you use them consistently, topic sentences provide a quick check that can ensure that all paragraphs of a section of text fit together in the most logical sequence.

It is vital, though, as with all aspects of your thesis, to remember that topic sentences change and develop as your thesis unfolds. Even if the topic sentence is perfect in one draft of your thesis, it may need some adjustment later.[3] Carefully worded topic sentences can also alert you that a paragraph is better placed somewhere else in your thesis.

28. Be wary of summary sentences

While the previous pointer was about beginning paragraphs, this pointer focuses on the end of your paragraphs. Summary sentences are another component recommended in guidebooks to writing. This is because a summary sentence serves to reiterate the main point. This type of sentence can help your writing; in some cases, however, it sets you up as someone who simply likes to repeat themselves. There are ways that you can avoid such an identity. If your paragraph has a clear topic sentence, a summary sentence rarely adds anything extra to the text, and you should consider omitting it. Similarly, if your paragraph is very short, the reader doesn't need to be reminded about the main point. Yet summary sentences do have their uses. They are great at the end of the long and detailed argument to bring points together for the reader. They remind your reader of what the text is about to help them better understand it. After an extra-long paragraph of special importance to your thesis, or at the end of the final paragraph of a longish section, a summary sentence helps the reader focus on the details that you want them to remember.

An alternative to a summary sentence is a final sentence in your previous paragraph that signposts to your reader how you are going to move your ideas forward. The topic sentence of the following paragraph can then be used to provide greater detail.

Sometimes summary sentences (and topic sentences) can create conflicts within supervision teams. If you come from a culture where you prefer summary sentences over topic sentences (or vice versa), talk over the issue with your supervisor(s). If your supervisor(s) come from a English-speaking background, you might want your summary sentence to appear in your initial drafts in bold font, so that they can read it first and then know where you are going. Sometimes it is useful to outline your intentions (and the cultural or linguistic reasons for it) in your introductory chapter so that your readers know why you are writing as you do. For further information about introductory chapters, see Pointer 16.

A summary sentence can have other uses that may appeal to those of you who have a strong editing identity. If you think about summary sentences as temporary scaffolding, you can write a summary sentence for every paragraph in your thesis with the aim of using this summary sentence to check the accuracy and consistency of the points raised in your paragraph. You can then delete some or all of these summary sentences, assured that you have written a good paragraph.

29. Footnotes and appendices to tuck away information

Even when you have paragraphs with carefully constructed topic and summary sentences, trying to restrict a paragraph to one point is often difficult in thesis writing as you have so much to say about everything. Footnotes allow you to store valuable content away from the main text so that you can stay focused on what is central to your argument now. Footnotes help you perform a 'tidy' researcher identity.[4]

If you are worried about excess footnotes, you needn't be. In the end, most of your footnotes will be temporary because the points will either seem less important in subsequent drafts and you will delete many of them; or they will seem more important, and you will elaborate these points elsewhere in the body of your thesis.

Another way of filtering information out of your paragraph so that you can focus on one point at a time is to allocate important information to appendices. In some disciplines that use footnotes and endnotes for referencing purposes (e.g., history, law, archaeology), extraneous information tends to be placed in appendices.[5] They can be useful in all disciplines. Appendices can be used to situate any information that you think readers might like to follow up on. They are useful for providing additional evidence of procedures described in your methodology chapter. Your appendices might include tables of data that are not central to your argument. For example, you might include a summary in your main text and additional information that you drew on to make this claim in an appendix. Background information (ethics forms, interview schedules) as well as transcripts are also useful appendices.

Before you write longer more complicated paragraphs, think about tucking some information into a footnote or an appendix. Think of footnotes and appendices as places where you can provide helpful extra information to those potential readers who would like to see more.

30. Tips on writing sentences for impact

Another consideration when structuring paragraphs is the structure of your sentences. Comments we made earlier about paragraph length are relevant for sentence length. Strings of long sentences (over four lines long) can be difficult for many readers to understand easily. To get your main point across, you might want to shorten a few of your sentences. Similarly, if you are someone who typically writes short sentences, you might want to lengthen a few sentences to avoid looking dull and list-like.

Varying a few of your sentence structures is effective for bringing out key ideas. If a key idea in your paragraph is represented in a short sentence (with only one verb), this sentence stands out from the rest of the text and your reader will focus on its content in the same way as if you raised your voice. This will enable you to get your main point across to your reader so that surrounding longer sentences become more effective. A carefully organized long sentence in a string of shorter ones has a similar effect. It makes its content appear visibly more important than the rest of the paragraph.

Essentially anything that bends grammatical rules can be used for impact. Words like 'But' or 'And' or 'So' don't usually appear at the beginning of a sentence. When used at the beginning of a sentence, they can make your sentences yell out at your reader. Yelling may not always be appropriate behavior, so think carefully before you make regular use of these words as the first words in your sentences. *Italics* is another way of drawing attention to a particular word or idea in a sentence. Italic font is a particularly good device when you are struggling to make a word, concept or idea prominent in your text,[6] or when you want the reader to be able to easily find it (e.g., when it is a key term). While such devices do have their purposes, if used often, they will lose their effect. Think about reserving perhaps one or two of these devices for your concluding chapter, when you want to bring home one final message to your reader.

There is yet another way of thinking about writing sentences for impact. Many readers consider what is presented first as most important. For example, in the sentence 'I wrote another draft after I consulted with my supervisor', the writing of another draft is viewed as the most important point. However, in the sentence 'After I consulted with my supervisor, I wrote another draft', the visit to the supervisor is the most relevant point. When editing your sentences, think carefully about the order of your ideas, and whether they convey the importance of what you are trying to say.

Most writing books give an array of advice about presenting information that you may or may not find useful. Advice often includes the avoidance of certain sentences such as 'there are four main points' because the expression 'there are' contains no meaningful information. A more useful start would be 'The four main points are…', since this structure helps you get straight to the point. But this advice isn't useful for everyone. The way you write depends on your identity as a writer. If you are someone who likes to bring points slowly into the text, you may prefer the 'there are' option.

Many writing books also recommend that you use passive sentences sparingly (e.g., 'The theory was developed by….'). The reasoning behind this advice again relates to the ways that information is presented to your reader. A passive sentence presents known information first (e.g., the study was completed by…), demoting new information to later in the sentence. Passive sentences can distract western-trained English-speaking readers who tend to look for the main point before they focus on other things. If you find putting the main idea first is too direct for your liking, feel free to use passive sentences and consider other techniques to bring out your key ideas (e.g., headings and/or topic sentences). There is always more than one way to express an idea.

For further reading, you might like Chapter 7 of Durkin's (2012) discussion of tips on maintaining coherence in your writing or Strunk and Tenney's (2000) classic advice on writing conventions. For something more thought-provoking, Pinker (2015) provides a readable guide for those who like to write outside traditional boundaries and Straus (2012) engages with dilemmas faced by international students when organizing their thoughts when English is their additional language.

31. Is your thesis reporting on the past or engaging in the present?

You *will complete* a thesis. You are *completing* a thesis. You *have completed* your thesis.

Which framing do you use when you write your thesis – the present, past or future? For some parts of your thesis, you may use all three. An introductory chapter describes what drove your interest in completing your thesis (a past event), why you think it is important to pursue this interest (a present circumstance), and your plans for making it happen (a future ideal).

In other instances, choices as to which tense you could use depend entirely on you. If you like to feel in control, using the present tense helps. The present tense (I analyze) can sound more certain than the future (I will analyze). The past tense can make your presence in the text sound more distant and reserved than the present tense.

Sometimes the way you understand your text will affect the tenses that you use. If you consider your literature review primarily as a chapter that reflects your current thinking, you might write it in the present tense. If you consider your literature review as a synopsis of what others have written on a particular topic, then you might choose to write it using the past tense. If you write your methodology as a procedure, you may use the present tense, if you write it as a summary of what you did and why, you will use the past tense. If you combine your findings and discussion into one chapter with the aim of analyzing rather than reporting, you might find it easier to write in the present tense. But these are not the only options.

Differences in your perspective also affect the tense you use. Do you see your results and their analysis as in the here-and-now or do you see them as having been based on information that you have collected and analyzed in the past? The decision here is a personal one based on how you wish to perform the text. Some thesis writers feel more comfortable using the present tense, others are more comfortable reporting in the past. The decision of which tense to use is ultimately yours. It is a good idea, however, to be explicit about your decisions with your supervisory team to ensure that everyone is thinking about (and editing) your text in the same way.

Often your tenses change as your thesis progresses. Your tenses in your methodology chapter are a case in point. In your early work, your methodology chapter is conceived as a proposal for work; in other words, work that is yet to be completed. You could write it in the past, a potential tense that you might use in this chapter. If this makes you feel as if you are lying, you might want to use a future-oriented word such as 'will' to signal tasks that are yet to be done, and then remove 'will' from your text as your thesis progresses. One advantage of the latter approach is that you can later do a word search for 'will' in your Word document and check whether you really did what you said you would do.[7]

Tense is also dependent on the genre in which you are writing your thesis. If you write your thesis as a story, there are choices you can make about what tense you want to use. The present tense can help bring your text to life, the past tense can make it sound a little more serious.

32. Your words matter! Nouns: the fewer, the better, but choose them wisely!

There was a time in school, where you might have been asked to label a word as a noun, a verb, or some other part of speech. You might have thought of the task as fun or perhaps you thought of it as boring or even confusing. You probably didn't consider the task as one that was particularly useful for life-long learning. However, it might have been more useful than you think as different word types have different functions, and understanding those functions has the potential to make your text (and you as a thesis writer) more or less powerful, and/or more or less convincing. If you understand how different types of words work, you can use this knowledge to craft your overall text to perform an identity as a confident academic writer, and a skillful researcher.

Nouns are important as they are used to represent things in the real world (e.g., a *survey* is a noun, it refers to a type of data collection). The idea here is each noun represents one thing and because of this, no two nouns refer to the same thing. This has implications for your thesis. Whenever you use a technical or key word in your argument, you need to ensure that you are consistent and only use that 'word'.[8] For example, a careful academic writer would never state that they are undertaking a *survey*, and later refer to it as a *questionnaire*. It adds confusion as some readers will see the two words as identical, others will see the two words as potentially similar, and some will see them as very different. A strong academic writer chooses nouns carefully (see also the discussion of definitions in Pointer 17), and consistently. If you use two different nouns just to vary your prose, your supervisor(s) and/or examiner(s) will invariably ask you to explain how those two nouns differ. If you are using different nouns to refer to the same thing, your readers may also feel that you don't know what you are talking about or that you do not have a good understanding of your field – an identity you never want as a thesis writer.

Your choice of nouns can send other messages. They can say a lot about who you are to your readers. In some instances, your choice of nouns can indicate whether you like to adopt new trends or take a more conservative approach to research. The choice of some nouns can even send messages about how you feel about your research and your place in it. As an example, three nouns, 'participants, informants, subjects', convey different messages about you as a user of these nouns. 'Participants' is a newer, inclusive term. The use of the term 'participants' can imply that you think a certain way about the people that you are interacting with. It can imply that you are someone who likes to do research with, rather than research for, or research on (Cameron et al., 1992). The term 'participant' is open enough to allow you to consider yourself as an insider while the terms 'informant' and 'subject' distance you. An 'informant' or 'subject' tends to be viewed as taking a more passive role in the research.

In some theses, you might be one of the participants/subjects/informants in your research. How would you like to label yourself? Such a question might help you decide on at least some of the nouns that you wish to use in your thesis.

Choose all your nouns carefully.

33. Verbs: Powerful friends, horrible enemies

In the case of verbs, our advice is very different. While it is wise to repeat the same nouns, you should embrace a diverse range of verbs as this part of speech helps you to reflect subtleties in your thinking (e.g., 'am I stating, discussing, summarizing, explaining or critiquing?').[9] Verbs indicate the strength of your initial ideas (e.g., 'I wondered, I believed, I questioned…'). They demonstrate your opinions about what you have read (e.g., 'I disagree with, I am concerned about, I am confused over…'). They allow you to frame your interpretation of how various authors contribute to prior research in your literature review (e.g., 'the authors pose a question, the authors mention a point (in passing), the authors state a claim, or authors argue for/against a point'). They also allow you to show both the strengths and the weaknesses of prior research (e.g., 'while I applaud the author's attempt to…, I disagree with…'). Throughout the thesis, verbs are particularly good at helping you to frame your argument (e.g., 'I concur with, I disagree with, I claim/posit that…/support x's findings').

In other words, when it comes to verbs, they are particularly good at distinguishing the contributions other researchers have made from your unique contribution to knowledge within the field. They help you to distinguish between what you think and what others have written. They place you in your research and show where you belong. Use them wisely. They empower you to perform a strong researcher identity, one that portrays you as an expert on a particular topic in your field. Adjectives and adverbs can also empower you. See Pointer 35 for further details.

Bloom's expanded taxonomy is a useful starting point for understanding more about verbs. This taxonomy divides verbs into different types depending on the depth of thinking that you want to convey about the topic. Anderson et al. (2001) provide a detailed account of Bloom's taxonomy.

34. Being an expert: using modal verbs for effect (words such as 'can, may, might')

A thesis is a piece of research that enables you to demonstrate to the world that you are an expert in a particular area of research (no matter how small). So, you need to sound like an expert. To perform this identity, you need to ensure that you state your positioning on things that matter.

A small set of verbs ('modal verbs') that precede the main verb in a clause help clarify your position (e.g., 'can/could, may might'). They give information to your reader about how sure you are about the information you are presenting in your thesis.

Because many modal verbs suggest that you are unsure, they are best avoided in your literature review, methodology and results, when the information you are presenting is unambiguous. Using modal verbs in these chapters of your thesis can give you a less confident voice. When you have a complete initial draft of your literature review and methodology chapters, you might want to do a search for modal verbs. By deleting some modal verbs, you can present yourself as more confident and knowledgeable both about your claims on how you fit in the literature and about your methodological decision-making.[10] You may not want to delete all your modal verbs as you may want to suggest, at times, that you are a little unsure. You don't want to sound like Donald Trump, certain about everything all the time.

Modal verbs are helpful in other parts of your thesis where you need to perform a speculative identity. As a thesis writer speculating on findings in your discussion and conclusion, modal verbs allow you to present information as not entirely conclusive. This may be because you (in hindsight or because of time constraints) might have not employed the 'perfect' methodology or because you are not entirely confident that there is only one potential interpretation of your findings. Modal verbs can be useful for nuancing, positioning and speculating on your weaker claims. In this context, the use of modal verbs allows you to perform an authoritative voice, that your readers will find hard to dispute.

Modal verbs have one additional use. In today's increasingly inclusive world, they can be used to reflect choice. Throughout this book, we have made extensive and deliberate use of modal verbs when giving advice to reinforce our positioning that we do not believe in a one-stop guide to thesis writing.

35. Being cautious and being assertive: Adjectives and adverbs

Your choice of adjectives and adverbs, which come in different types, also play a role in establishing your identity in your thesis. Some adjectives enable you to perform a cautious identity (e.g., 'the results are tentative/inconclusive/confusing etc.'), one which can be quite useful when the findings from your thesis are somewhat unclear. However, if you use these devices in a sentence with a modal verb ('may/can' etc.), you can appear as if you have almost nothing to say (e.g., 'the findings may show tentative insights') about both the nature of your data and your own ability to interpret it. Being too cautious is not necessarily a good researcher identity.

Other adjectives have the opposite effect. They point to the strength of your data or analysis (e.g., 'the results are conclusive, overwhelming etc.'). When you want to emphasize a point, these adjectives are useful ones to draw on.

While adjectives describe things (i.e., data, findings, analysis), adverbs describe the quality of actions (i.e., 'show clearly, prove irrefutably'). When manner adverbs (e.g., 'clearly, powerfully' etc.) are carefully combined with well-chosen verbs, they give you a powerful voice (e.g., 'The authors *rightly* argue their position; the authors *strongly* refute a position.').

Other adverbs that may initially appear powerful are not. This is because some adverbs (particularly quantitative adverbs (e.g., 'a lot of, very') are traditionally associated with unempowered speech, and their use has the potential to project that identity onto the writer. One way of avoiding this identity is to avoid such adverbs. There is a very simple reasoning behind this association. Generalized adverbs are difficult to explain. What makes something 'very important' or 'very relevant' rather than just 'important' or 'relevant'? The content of academic text needs to be accurate. It's important to use words that you can justify.

36. Authorship: when to use a personal pronoun, 'I/we'

Writing is, at its very core, a form of self-expression,[11] an expression of your thinking. Yet teachers of composition often recommend that if you use a first-person pronoun in your writing, you do so sparingly. This is partly because a key part of understanding writer identity is knowing how explicit to be about inputting aspects of yourself into your writing. When you write 'Starks and Macdonald (2022) provide a *clear* definition of a *key* concept', the words 'clear' and 'key' present the authors' interpretation that the description is 'clear' and that the concept is, in fact, 'key'. To add expressions such as 'I think' or 'we think'[12] when elaborating on the above text would be redundant.

In some cases, whether you use 'I' (or 'we' if writing a thesis by/with one or more co-authored publications) depends on the surrounding text. Expressions such as 'I disagree' can be redundant, but it might not always be. If you want to truly dispute a fact, 'I disagree' might come in handy as it has the potential to yell out to your audience that this is your thinking and in what follows, you will write an argument on a particular topic that you have strong opinions about. The use of 'I' with a strong opinion verb conveys information on how you wish the text to be read.

In other instances, a first-person pronoun can be used to give you control over your argument. Think about differences between 'The three issues are' and 'My three issues are…'. The use of the personal pronoun 'my' shows the reader that you are making selective choices. In other words, it's not every issue under consideration here; it's three points of *my* choosing. It's important to remember, however, that if you use 'my' (or 'our') to restrict your data in this way, you need to state why you are doing so, perhaps in a footnote. See Pointer 29 on the use of footnotes.

The examples discussed thus far are cases where you use one instance of the personal pronoun to make a point. In other circumstances in your thesis, you may use the personal pronoun 'I' throughout the text to achieve an entirely different range of outcomes. The personal pronoun 'I' scattered throughout a section of text can have the effect of making your text more inviting. Some readers find that introducing 'I' into your text makes it more enjoyable to read. This can be especially true in your introductory chapter.

A first-person pronoun can have different functions in different chapters of your thesis. You may use 'I' in your introduction to tell a story to illustrate a point. Throughout your methodology chapter, you may use 'I' (or 'we') to help the reader follow you on your research journey, as you detail where you went, what you did and how (irrespective of the genre in which you write your chapter).

In some ways, how you use 'I/our' in your thesis is an individual decision as not all graduate researchers will feel uncomfortable if they use 'I' throughout their thesis. Whether and how you use a first-person pronoun can also be discipline-based. Not all fields of study regularly use the first-person pronoun when writing up a methodology (Taylor and Goodall, 2019). Have a discussion in a supervision meeting about how you would like to proceed. The question may not be 'Should I use the pronoun "I" in my thesis?' but 'How should I use "I" in my thesis?'.

For a more detailed analysis of the uses of the pronoun 'I' in student writing in business, check out Taylor and Goodall (2019). For further reading into the ways that you can increase and diminish your authoritative voice as an author, you might want to read Hyland's (2002) early work which contains ample illustrative examples of stance taking and a discussion of why particular stances might be difficult for those who have English as an additional language.

37. Gendered pronouns and the political self

While many thesis writers at some point contemplate whether to use pronouns such as 'I' or 'we', other pronouns have recently come under the spotlight. It is now increasingly commonplace to nominate your third-person pronouns on websites and in job applications. Options include gender binary choices ('he/him, she/her') as well as a range of neo-pronouns, e.g., 'they/their, ze/zir, xe/xem etc'. Your choices reflect your positioning on this issue as well as how you wish to position the authors cited in your thesis.

Because 'who you are' is always multiple (cultural, academic, engendered etc.), some writers are upfront about their gender and may even offer a range of acceptable options (e.g., 'they/she') that can be used to refer to them. Others choose to leave their gendered identity unspecified altogether because they may not see it as part of their identity as an academic.

In today's world, which is increasingly grappling with diversity and inclusion, the wide range of choices can create uncertainties as to how to best represent researchers in your field in your academic writing. Which pronoun/s (if any) are you going to use to identify the authors you cite in your thesis? Your initial decisions could change as you learn more about the individuals within your field and the various pronouns they use to self-identify themselves in their research. There are no easy answers as any pronoun use has embedded within it a political stance.

For some of you, you may take a conservative approach and choose to use the classic binary 'he' or 'she' when citing authors throughout your thesis. A binary choice is relatively easy to implement as most names are gender-specific. There will only be a few gender-neutral names (e.g., 'Ashley, Kim, Jordan, Wei, Minh' etc.) and names that are unknown to you that may cause you difficulties. This choice remains the unmarked option for many writers, and for many researchers, it is relatively uncontroversial at least for now.

It's important to realize, however, that what may appear uncontroversial now, may not read that way in the future. Your thesis will be available long after you complete your candidature. We don't know if the use of binary pronouns will be something that will be looked down on in decades to come. We can't predict the future so you shouldn't spend a lot of time on this. Our advice is to make a decision that makes you feel comfortable now. If you want to cite your thesis at some future point in time, you can always paraphrase your work if your preferred pronoun use has changed.

If you are someone who feels uncomfortable with the binary options, here are some non-binary ones that are used now that you might consider, as well as their potential drawbacks. One commonly used option is to opt out of the debate altogether. When it comes to pronoun use, you can refer to 'the writer/author/researcher' and use the associated pronoun, 'they' (e.g., 'the writer acknowledges...., they do so by....').[13] While this option may sound appealing, 'the writer/author/researcher' and its associated pronoun 'they' implicitly distance you from the author's work and can make you sound less interested in what they have to say. If your writer identity wants to connect with your reader, this pronoun choice may not be the best option for you.

Another option is for you to take a somewhat intermediate position. You could use pronouns 'she/her' and 'he/him' as unmarked pronouns and explain the occasional use of another pronoun if a particular author who you are citing prefers to be otherwise addressed. While this choice may sound inviting, it can be a difficult one to implement as it requires time to find the appropriate pronoun. Potential sources of knowledge – such as the author's website – may not always provide such information. The question you need to ask is how important is it for your researcher identity to spend time sourcing information on pronoun use? If you believe that it is important for you to use pronouns your cited authors prefer, you need to be willing to take time to check pronouns on websites (perhaps towards the end of your candidature, when you may not always have a lot of spare time).

There are additional options to consider when your cited authors use pronouns that are not used by all of society. Referring to others using a third-person neo-pronoun such as 'they' (singular) or 'ze' can bring into the open an identity that is still hidden in some contexts. It can also openly position you in the politics of diversity.

Another issue to consider is the rules for using neo-pronouns. If using neo-pronouns, you need to use them appropriately (Devine, 2022). In the LGBIQ+ community, when 'they' refers to a singular author, it takes a singular verb (e.g., 'they notes'), when 'they' refers to two or more authors (e.g., 'Starks and Robertson'), the pronoun 'they' takes a plural verb (e.g., 'they note…'). These differences in the use of 'they' pronouns can create paragraphs with combinations of sentences such as 'They *considers* this idea to be interesting' and 'They *consider* this idea to be interesting'. Other neo-pronouns have different grammatical patterning. 'Xe' has singular verb agreement ('Xe also considers this idea'). There are also subtle meaning differences. 'Xe' is not a substitute for 'they'. The two neo-pronouns are not synonymous.

Another option that you can explore is to spell out all possibilities for every author, but this may offer other challenges to parts of your identity as a thesis writer. How do you feel about phrases such as 'she or he or they etc.' or contractions such as 's/he and they etc.'? Because a thesis writer identity tends to strive for consistency and conciseness, some thesis writers may find these long lists of pronouns somewhat disconcerting. If you take this option, there are additional considerations. You will also need to consider the order in which such a list is written (e.g., 'they, s/he, he etc.'). What is presented first is often implicitly seen as of greater importance.

In contexts where you are writing on gender equality, you could take a progressive approach, and use 'they singular' or 'ze/xe' or some other neo-pronoun everywhere.

No matter what your choice is, we recommend that as an academic writer, it is useful to be explicit about everything you write. Given the plethora of options for referring to your cited authors, we suggest that you explain your pronoun use to your reader in your introductory chapter (whatever your choice). This explanation can even be in a footnote (see Pointer 29 for a discussion of footnotes).

If the preceding paragraphs in this pointer are causing you some distress, you can breathe a sigh of relief as other decisions about pronouns are easier to make. As a thesis writer, you may wish to refer to your preferred pronoun in the title page of your thesis, e.g., 'Donna Starks (she/her)'. This addition of pronouns is optional. You don't need to indicate your pronouns on the title page of your thesis. Some of you may not wish to identify your preferred pronouns in your personal world to your academic world. The decision is yours. It is your thesis; you have the ultimate control over how you wish to identify yourself within it. Elsewhere in your thesis, there is only one pronoun to describe you, and this pronoun 'I' is the same for everyone. Whether you use the pronoun 'I' in your thesis is your choice (see Pointer 37 for some thoughts about the use of 'I' in your thesis).

For an in-depth discussion of gender-neutral pronouns, their history and how they relate to issues of inclusion, see Baron (2020). For insights into how 'they (sg)' be taught to English as additional language learners, see Speyer and Schleef (2019). Devine's (2022) website on gender-neutral pronouns provides a range of useful details on pronoun use and why it is important to try to be gender-inclusive in your spoken discourse.

38. Things that don't 'really' matter (that much)!

We end with a few things that most of you shouldn't dwell on. English is a language that not everyone speaks and writes in the same way. For most of you, regional differences in English will not even register as important in your thesis writing and will only cause minor anxiety when you and your supervisors disagree on which forms of language to use. There are some exceptions. You may have a strong sense of national identity and may want to spend time ensuring that your grammatical identity is consistent with your national identity. If you are writing a thesis that has strong national overtones (e.g., a topic in British history), you may also want to think about whether the regional variety of English that you use is an appropriate reflection of the content of your thesis.

Words, spelling

Some words are used in some parts of the world more than others. Most of these words have little bearing on your thesis. For example, does it really matter if you conducted your study 'in the fall of 2022' or 'in the autumn of 2022'? Most people know that 'fall' and 'autumn' have similar meanings, with one term preferred by speakers who have learned American-based varieties of English and the other by those who have learned British-based varieties of English. See Trudgill & Hannah (2017) for a list of differences between English varieties.

Some regional differences in English language use can be contentious if you are a thesis writer who believes that there can be only one correct form. For example, did you know that the plural of *evidence,* can be either *evidences* or *evidence* and that for some individuals *'conversate'* and *'opine'* are 'real' words but for others, they are not? If members of your supervisory team disagree, come to a decision about what to use if you or your supervisor(s) introduce a word or grammatical form that is unfamiliar to some members of the supervisory team, and then move on to more important stuff.

Spelling also differs from one place to the next but the differences are often less than clear. Even if you want to use ways of writing traditionally associated with American or British English, you are in for a losing battle. Globalization has affected the English language. Spellings that were originally 'British English' or 'American English' are no longer so cut and dry. 'Analyze' with a 'z' is now common practice for some writers of British English (see Trudgill & Hannah, 2017) and some varieties of English, such as Canadian English, have long preferred bits of both British and American English (*'analyze'* and *'colour'*). Some spelling conventions are confusing. Australian English has a political system that has a 'Labor Party', but they fight for 'fair labour'. For most of you, there are more important things than spelling to consider when you write your thesis. This means that you can opt to use 'colour-coding' or 'color-coding' in your thesis. In most instances, all that really matters is that you are consistent and once you spell a word in your thesis, you spell it the same way all the time. You shouldn't spell 'colour' in one chapter and 'color' in another. You don't need to think about regional varieties of English if you don't want to. If you opt for 'colour-coding', you can still write 'analyze' with the 'z' rather than with an 's'. It's your choice! There are only a couple of things to note. To remain faithful to the voice of your cited authors, words inside quotes should retain the original spelling of the authors. Their book/article/chapter/journal titles in your reference list should also be true to the authors' spelling. This may mean that you may use different sorts of spelling in some of your quotes and some bibliographical details in your reference list. A second note concerns a few select words where you may not have a choice. 'Honors/Honours' may be one word that you might like to check if you are completing your Hono(u)rs degree. 'Program/programme' is another word that you might want to think carefully about. Your university may specify the preferred or requisite spelling of these words in the template for the title page of your thesis.

Grammar

Varieties of English also differ in their grammar. Sometimes, whole sets of words differ. Words that denote groups (e.g., 'team, group, university') are an example. A group can be seen as a single entity, but it can also be seen as an entity that contains multiple things within it. When the grammatical focus is on how any group contains more than one thing, the accompanying verb is plural ('the research team are'). When the grammatical focus is on the unitary nature of groups, the accompanying verb will play along and a singular verb will be used (e.g., 'the research team is').[14] Such differences in English grammar in different varieties of English can cause confusion if members of the supervisory team differ in their use. When differences arise, note them and agree on a common usage and everything will be relatively straightforward from there.

Some grammar differences can be trickier as they are largely unconscious differences. Prepositions (e.g., 'in, at, on') can cause frustration if members of your team have different writing practices. For example, did you complete your research 'in a particular location' or 'at a particular location'? Your choice may depend on where you are from, or where you were schooled, or even what your parents used to say. Phrasal verbs are also particularly prone to variation. When you are writing a thesis, are your results 'different *than*/ different *to*/different *from* other research in the field'? Don't assume you are wrong just because your supervisor gives you an alternative word. The bottom line is do not waste time arguing about what is 'correct', make a decision and stick with it.

Punctuation

Many people have strong views about correct and incorrect punctuation, partly because most people are not aware of the options. Traditionally British punctuation placed any punctuation after 'quotation marks', and American orthographic conventions did the 'reverse.' The positioning of footnote numbering and punctuation is another traditional difference between varieties of English. When a name ends in 's', as in Starks, Jones etc. the possessive used to be 'Starks's/ Jones's ideas' in British-based varieties of English, but 'Starks'/Jones' ideas' in American-based varieties of English. Our advice is to be consistent and write in the way that you feel comfortable. Since punctuation differences are less conscious than many other differences in language use, if you decide to change to your supervisor(s)' conventions (or you are working on a thesis by/with publication as part of a team), ensure any changes are consistent throughout your thesis and explain this to all concerned so that the team is using the same set of rules. It is very easy to be inconsistent with punctuation when multiple authors contribute to the text and when your focus is on more important things such as the content of your thesis.

Language is ever-changing and differs from one person to the next. Some punctuation differences are the result of older versus newer writing conventions. Abbreviations of Latin phrases (*exempli gratiā* 'for the sake of example' or *id est* 'that is' are cases in point). Abbreviations of these Latin phrases (e.g. and i.e.) have two full stops, one after each Latin word. The problem is: these abbreviations have long lost their associations with their original Latin phrases and the punctuation rules have become obscured. So while the traditional forms were with full stops, some style guides may tell you something different.[15] Other disappearing punctuation includes full stops after titles (Dr. or Dr), and commas used to conjoin clauses (e.g., 'I completed the data gathering, and started to analyze the data', or 'I completed my data gathering and started to analyze the data'). Have a chat if you notice that your supervisory team are suggesting you use their preferred punctuation. You don't want to make a change in one sentence and leave other sentences elsewhere in your thesis unchanged.

Other language issues

Examiners are often asked to reflect on the quality of your written text and whether it meets academic standards. Your supervisors are likely to ask you to remove language from your thesis that is not considered to be standard academic English. Non-standard language is not wrong, it is just not deemed appropriate for a thesis. Non-standard ways of writing include new forms of language. Two examples of newer writing conventions are the spelling of 'their' as 'there' and the non-standard use of ('s) to mark a plural ('one chapter/two chapter's'). For some of you, your grammatical self will be pulling your hair out at even the thought of mixing these up. For others, you may be saying, that's me! If you don't distinguish the plural and the possessive, you should be comforted to know that you are not alone. People all over the world are writing in the same way as you. For a discussion of the plural/possessive check out Lukač (2014). The reason such changes take place is two-fold. First, one of the forms is relatively rare so you don't use that form often. 'There' and the plural (without the apostrophe) are much more common than 'their' and the possessive (with the apostrophe). Second, the two forms are used in different ways in a sentence. This means that using the 'wrong' form doesn't affect comprehension. Everyone still understands what you have written. In other words, the possessive apostrophe and the different spellings of 'their/there' have relatively little use. Still, the new non-standard form may irk your supervisor's (sg.) (or supervisors' (pl.)), or your graduate school's grammatical identity. For someone who doesn't use the newer forms, it appears to them as if you have made a mistake (used the wrong word). For this reason, we wouldn't suggest you write any new forms of English in your thesis. It's far too dangerous when you are graded on your academic English.

If you are someone who can't tell the difference between 'there/their' and the plural 's' and the possessive 's', the forms are the same in your head. This means that you will find it very difficult to identify and change them, even when you are told the rules. Don't get frustrated. Ask a friend who hates the merger (i.e., a person who uses the traditional words in a traditional way) to check your use. You might have an English as an additional language writer check these words in your thesis. Individuals who have been explicitly taught a language are often acutely aware of any grammar uses that 'break' their taught rules.

For further reading on differences between British and American English, Scott (2004) provides a summary of the classic differences. Peter Trudgill and Jean Hannah (2017) provide long lists of differences found in a broader range of varieties of English.

Notes

1   Headings are useful for creating hyperlinked navigation. By creating a Table of Contents, you can obtain a quick overview of the topics covered and their relative positioning in the text to discover what might be missing.
2   The length of a heading is a very individual thing. Although it varies from one person to another, keep in mind that headings should be succinct. They should index, not explain.
3   Poorly written topic sentences can be worse than no topic sentence at all. Topic sentences should state what the point of the paragraph is and tell the reader how to read the paragraph. If there is a disconnect between the topic sentence and the rest of the paragraph, no matter how small, this can affect the readability of the paragraph. For this reason, we recommend that the order of points in your topic sentence should be presented in the order that they appear in the paragraph.
4   Endnotes and footnotes are a great way of stopping examiners from asking questions as they read. Footnotes can be used to explain personal choices (e.g., they can be used to explain why you excluded certain data or results, or why you chose to introduce a particular type of argument or literature). They can also be used to highlight potential incongruities in your text (e.g., the use 'I' and 'we', if writing a thesis by/with publication) or explain your reasons for writing or thinking.
5   Appendices and Appendixes are both accepted as the plural of Appendix. See Pointer 39 for other writing conventions that are not 'that' important when writing your thesis.
6   Bold font stands out a little too much and can disrupt reader flow.
7   At this point you might reread the surrounding text and see if you need to add more points into your methodology chapter. You will find that there will likely be points that you have forgotten to mention in the first draft.
8   While academic writing tends to look down on repetition, this is not the case when using nouns.
9   You should not use a thesaurus or the word search function to find a verb with the same meaning if that word is not part of your existing vocabulary as verbs can have different nuances. Word search functions are handy if you feel that you haven't got the 'right' verb to express your ideas and you are searching for alternative (known) words that might better express your thoughts.
10 Historically, the past tense of 'can' and 'may' was 'could' and 'might'. In present-day English you can use both in the same context (e.g., 'I can analyze the data'/'I could analyze the data'). In many cases, the difference is one of positioning.

The historical past tense 'could' and 'might' positions the writer persona further from their text, whereas the use of 'can' and 'may' has the opposite effect. If you wish to appear more actively engaged in the text, you might want to use 'can, may, will' intend of 'could, might, would'.

11 For a detailed analysis of stance and voice in academic writing and the ambiguities, difficulties and fluidities involved, check out Hyland and Guinda (2019).

12 If you are part of a research team where part of your thesis is by/with publication, you may want to use 'we' to refer to researchers even when the publication is single-authored. If you are completing a traditional thesis, it may be best to avoid 'we', as this pronoun when used to represent a single author has the effect of distancing the author from their text.

13 An academic voice is a consistent voice. For this reason, it is not advisable to use a gender-specific pronoun in some contexts, and a gender-neutral 'they' pronoun in other contexts if there is no stated reason for doing so.

14 You may find that not all words pattern consistently as language often changes one word at a time. For a more detailed analysis of how language is changing worldwide, we recommend Bauer (2014).

15 You should check with your university for any stylesheet that you need to follow.

References

Anderson, Lorin W., et al. (2001). *A taxonomy for learning, teaching and assessing: A revision of Bloom's taxonomy of educational objectives*. Longman.

Baron, Dennis. (2020). *What's your pronoun? Beyond he and she*. Liveright Publishing, A Division of W.W. Norton.

Bauer, Laurie. (2014). *Watching English change: An introduction to the study of linguistic change in Standard Englishes in the twentieth century*. Routledge.

Cameron, Deborah, et al. (1992; reprinted Ebook 2020). *Researching language: Issues of power and method*. Routledge.

Devine, Norelle. (July 2022). Gender-neutral pronouns 101: Everything you've always wanted to know. https://www.them.us/story/gender-neutral-pronouns-101-they-them-xe-xem

Durkin, Diane Bennett. (2012). *Writing strategies for the education dissertation*. Routledge.

Hyland, Ken (2002). Authority and invisibility: Authority and identity in academic writing. *Journal of Pragmatics, 34(8)*, 1091–1112. https://doi.org/10.1016/S0378-2166(02)00035-8

Hyland, Ken, & Guinda, Sancho Carmen (eds.), (2019). *Stance and voice in written academic genres*. Palgrave.

Lukač, M. (2014). Apostrophe(')s, who needs them?: A further invitation to contribute to questions studied by the 'Bridging the Unbridgeable' Project at the Leiden Centre for Linguistics. *English Today, 30(3)*, 3–4. https://doi.org/10.1017/S0266078414000200

Pinker, Steven. (2015). *The sense of style: A thinking person's guide to writing in the 21st century*. Penguin.

Scott, John Calvert. (2004). American and British business-related spelling differences. *Business Communication Quarterly*, *67*(2), 153–167. https://doi.org/10.1177/1080569904265424

Speyer, Lydia Gabriella, & Schleef, Erik. (2019). Processing 'gender-neutral' pronouns: A self-paced reading study of learners of English. *Applied Linguistics*, *40*(5), 793–815. https://doi.org/10.1093/applin/amy022

Strauss, Pat. (2012). 'The English is not the same': Challenges in thesis writing for second language speakers of English. *Teaching in Higher Education*, *17*(3), 283–293. https://doi.org/10.1080/13562517.2011.611871

Strunk, William J., & Tenney, Edward A. (2000). *The elements of style*. (4th ed.). Allyn & Bacon (Pearson).

Taylor, Helen, & Goodall, John. (2019). A preliminary investigation into the rhetorical function of 'I' in different genres of successful business student academic writing. *Journal of English for Academic Purposes*, *38*, 135–145. https://doi.org/10.1016/j.jeap.2019.01.009

Trudgill, Peter, & Hannah, Jean. (2017). *International English: A guide to varieties of English around the world*. (6th ed.). Taylor and Francis.

What could possibly go wrong?

Overview

It is rare to get through thesis writing without an interruption of some kind. While you are deeply immersed in your world of thesis writing, the rest of the world continues, sometimes in ways that you least expect. Things happen outside your control. They may be personal; your health as well as that of your family members may require attention. They may be academic i.e., staff retrenchment may lead to the loss of members of your supervisory team and in-person meetings may be replaced by online learning formats, all of which may exacerbate feelings of isolation. Negotiating life will almost certainly impact on your writing.

Even when everything in your personal life seems to be going fine, it's very easy to lose your centre, your focus. The intense and sometimes highly personal nature of thesis writing puts a lot of strain on you. Supervision and thesis timelines might be keeping you awake at night. You may lose confidence in your writing ability, and this may cause a loss of voice or writer's block; you may be beset with self-doubt. Feedback may be driving you insane. You may start to think that your thesis isn't saying anything (important), that you are incapable of finishing your thesis or that you don't want to finish it anymore.

This chapter considers six relatively common challenges you may face and pointers for how you can circumnavigate them. If you know in advance the possible pitfalls, then you can consider possible solutions before you get too distressed. You might be surprised at what opportunities can arise out of a crisis.

DOI: 10.4324/9781003323402-6

Figure 6.1   When your thesis hits the unexpected

39. Your personal life is a mess!

You've gained 10 kilos, have RSI and haven't laughed at a joke for months! These are all typical signs of stress. A little stress can be good, but too much becomes unproductive. When you are distressed, keeping a focus on writing is difficult. It's quite easy to let slip any attempts at maintaining your health. You have many possible reasons for not taking a break. It's too hot/cold to go for your regular run, or your running buddy is sick. You can't spare the time to take the kids to the park, visit your mother, or go on a date! If this sounds like you, you may be starting to lose your centre.

The first step to relocating your centre is to recognize you have a problem.[1] Take a moment to read Chapter 2 and try to focus on your personal priories and your inner circle of loved ones. Your friends and family may have been trying for months to let you know that you are a bit off-kilter. This might be the time to call in some help, someone to bring meals, someone to mind the children for a little while – or it might be a good time to hit the pause button for a couple of days to re-energize and reconnect with those you care about. Think about the advice you would give a friend if they were at risk of losing their centre. Would the advice work for you too?

There are different types of obstacles. Some relate to life in general. The health and well-being of a family member or close friend may be seriously compromised, and you need to take time out to spend with them, supporting them as best you can.

Sometimes it is your own well-being and health that has taken a downturn. Your health is your number one priority. If it is a minor medical issue, create a little time for yourself no matter how busy you feel, and attend to the things you have been advised to by your doctor. Try to spend an extra moment to do some gentle stretching, take a slow walk round the block. The fresh air will help. Breathe deep and slow. As noted in Chapter 2, it's amazing how slow breathing relaxes the brain so that you can think more clearly about what you are experiencing and find ways to overcome it. It's far less painful than continuing to bang your head into that brick wall! If your health issues are more serious, you might consider other options (see Pointer 44 on postponing your thesis).

Sometimes the issues are emotional ones. The stress and transformational aspects of a thesis can impact on relationships, even sometimes leading to their breakdown (Carter et al., 2013). If you have a partner, they may not appreciate the ways in which you are changing, your different priorities, or how busy you are. If you are a person with a disability, you may require support from someone who is not your primary caregiver, and it may be difficult for the primary caregiver to let go. Those of you with families from some traditional cultural backgrounds may find that family do not appreciate your new researcher identities, they may be afraid of how your changing identity impacts traditional family structures. If you have a child, they may feel that you are not spending enough time with them, and they may need more of your attention. If you have strong community commitments, and are having challenges meeting community needs, you can seek out advice from community leaders and elders. If you have a career, and you have increasing demands from your workplace, you might ask for a meeting to discuss the tensions. Perhaps there is a crisis at work, and you are urgently needed. You might want to discuss this with your supervisor(s) to work through possible options. If you are experiencing feelings of conflict between your thesis and any aspect of your personal life, you may be feeling emotionally depleted and that can lead to feelings of exhaustion (Hunter & Devine, 2016). If this is happening, try to take early action. Seeking help from those you trust is crucial, whether these are supervisors, others in the department, family friends or elders in your community. Whatever difficulties you are experiencing, don't leave issues to fester.

Work on keeping communication open. If you think you can't talk to family, friends or colleagues, you may need to find someone else you trust or seek out a counselling service to help you work through your issues. Sharing the problem with others in online forums where anonymity is practiced might provide you with emotional outlets and like-minded people who have been in similar situations. The thesiswhisperer.com is one well-established forum designed to raise issues and invite feedback.

In some instances, it may be useful to take some leave from thesis writing to sort things out or you might think about adjusting your studies to part-time for a couple of months (or longer) while you sort out your life.

40. Supervision

Being supervised is not easy, and there are many reasons for this. You may have thought you had the perfect supervision team, but time has revealed a gap between your expectations and reality. When you realize there is a problem, you need to take action because waiting and hoping for change doesn't fix anything. What might be a small problem initially can grow bigger if left unaddressed.

There are different ways that you can go about asking for change. Try to think through everything before you act. It can be hard to undo a sudden and ill-considered outburst. Your supervisor(s) may not even be aware that you are having difficulties.

Sometimes when your thesis changes direction, your existing supervisory team may not be able to offer you the support you need. While they might have been a great fit for your original thesis idea, they may not have expertise in specific areas, theories or methods that you now wish to use. If you feel that your thesis design no longer fits with their areas of expertise, try raising the issue as a general point about your needs in your supervisory session. Supervisors are unlikely to take this personally. They usually have your best interests at heart and may even feel relieved not to have to supervise a thesis on the topic they know little about, or a methodology that doesn't fit with their way of being and doing.

During your research journey, your needs change. You may require quite different forms of support, or different ways of working. Is there someone who can be added to your supervisory team who you think might help you if they have the interest and the availability? Some supervisors are very flexible with suggestions for changes to the supervisory team, others not so much.

You may be feeling that your supervisors are able to provide adequate and useful feedback, but you aren't getting enough advice or time from them (González-Betancor & Dorta-González, 2020). This can have a significant impact on feelings of well-being and personal self-worth. You need to be worried. Insufficient time with supervisors, along with unmet expectations, increases the likelihood that you will not finish your thesis. Think about whether this is a new issue. If a supervisor is suddenly having less time for you, could there potentially be things going on in their life that you are unaware of? Even supervisors are thrown life curveballs. Will an open and honest conversation get everything back on track? Did you keep a record of the initial agreement that your team reached about the mode and frequency of meetings, and can you use this now as a talking point to express your concern/disappointment/frustration?

If you are simply not getting along with a supervisor, perhaps have a quiet word with your other supervisor or the chair of your panel (if you have one) about a potential change. Would switching over your principal supervisor and co-supervisor, or maybe even adding another member to the team to help freshen things up? Talk these issues through with your supervisors, or, if this is not possible, take it to a higher level such as arranging a meeting with the person in your school/department who looks after supervision. They may be able to suggest options. Suffering in silence won't help you move forward to find a solution.

Another surprisingly common problem is that supervisors leave (usually at the most inconvenient moment for you). Some supervisors are asked to leave as part of a university restructure, others are offered a better job elsewhere, and some even retire. This can have a big impact, particularly on the direction of your research. It can be a positive or negative experience, depending on what action you take.

If you are an honors student with a single supervisor, talk with your graduate school coordinator or someone in your department who has oversight of supervision. They will know who is available to supervise. For master's and doctoral theses, most universities these days have built-in contingency plans. You may have lost just one supervisor and other members of your supervisory team can help fill the void. Hopefully your supervision team has been working well and is well briefed or already fully engaged in your work. Having a vacancy may present an opportunity to bring in someone new who has the skills and attitudes that will make a great positive contribution. Sometimes having a fresh start with new supervisor can have positive outcomes. Losing a supervisor can be an opportunity for you to take a stronger role in the shaping of your thesis in a different way.

Bringing in a new supervisor is going to be an adjustment for the entire supervisory team and talking through how the new configuration is going to work is important for all of you. You may know of someone who you might like as a supervisor (in your department or elsewhere in the university).[2] You could raise this idea with your team.

If you are very unlucky, you may have lost both your supervisors and found yourself orphaned. Or perhaps only one member of your supervisor team has left, but you believe that person is crucial to the success of your thesis. You might explore changing to another university, especially if you are at an early stage in your studies. It's important to talk with the department or faculty as they may be able to facilitate changes for you when there isn't a new supervisor for you at your current university. Before you set your heart on that, check the rules and regulations, especially if you are an international student with visa limitations. Some university have time limits on transferring students between universities, and clearly transfers involving international students are much more challenging. If you have a scholarship or other funding, this may not be a move for you. Changing universities is really a last-ditch option.

Sadly, whatever your needs and decisions, a new supervision team will mean that you need to learn to work in new ways as each supervisor has their own way of working. This will almost certainly mean that you need to reconsider prior agreements. It will also probably mean that you will need a little extra time to complete your thesis. Ask for any extra time earlier. The university will understand the potential effects of changes in supervision. In the turmoil, there is one upside. You have the opportunity to explain to someone new how the parts of your thesis fit together – something that may not have happened previously.

For further understandings of issues of losing supervisors, the consequences, and possible solutions, we suggest the article by Wisker and Robinson (2013).

41. Your timetable is out of sync!

Time, or rather the lack of it, is perhaps the most common problem facing thesis writers. This can occur at various stages in the thesis journey.

There are many ways that a thesis can get behind schedule. In the social sciences, changes to thesis design are common. You could be making a small shift of focus, or you could have decided to take on a completely new topic. You may have discovered that you are no longer interested in your chosen topic or that it has already been researched. You may change direction due to changes to your professional aspirations. After reading extensively, you may want to change your theoretical framework or methodology. A clearer focus often means that you will be more productive in the long run. If you spend an extra month or two reading, it's not something that you need to worry about.

You may feel that you have lost valuable time waiting for ethics approval. Conducting research safely is a priority for researchers and getting the necessary approvals to conduct your research often takes more time than anticipated. Your ethics application may require numerous revisions. If your ethics applications are delaying you, you may want to rethink your participant and data collection procedures. It's not the end of the world to change your research design. It may not be feasible to conduct a study with your optimal participants within the time frame of your thesis research. Try to be flexible. There is always the possibility of future research opportunities after your thesis is completed.

Another time delay often occurs during data collection. Your participants may be difficult to schedule, or they may drop out during data gathering. Consider whether having fewer participants will provide sufficient data for your thesis. Open communication with your supervisor(s) about how many participants are needed for a robust thesis can make for a useful conversation. What is optimal and what is realistic are entirely different issues.

After you have collected your data, transcription of interviews can be quite time-consuming. Think carefully about how much data you need transcribed. You might listen to the recordings and only select the participants that have the richest data. If you need more participant data later, you can transcribe relevant parts of the recordings. While learning how to transcribe is an important part of learning how to do research, if you have extensive transcription, you might want to talk to your supervisor(s) about delegating some transcription to others, perhaps a paid service.

Certain parts of your journey can be very demanding. Data analysis can be overwhelming, especially if you have a lot of data, in multiple forms and you are not quite sure which direction you will take. Rather than trying to tackle the whole task, try working with a small segment – perhaps a single participant's data – to see if your intended approach will work effectively.

Other delays can occur when you try to answer your research question. Even with careful initial consideration to your research question(s) and research design, your data does not always work in the ways that you anticipated. As an example, perhaps the responses in your interviews are vastly different or they do not provide a complete answer to your research question. You cannot go back and redo interviews or collect additional data. Think about what your existing data is telling you and potentially consider how to rework your research questions to align with your data. Sometimes small changes to the wording of your research questions can make a big difference. Sometimes you may find that it is more useful to cover only one of your original research questions. It's important to talk through changes with your supervisor(s) rather than worrying about it.

Yet another common time-related concern relates to your thesis structure itself. If you have chosen to write your thesis by/with publications and are encountering issues, talk with your supervisor(s) before you get really distressed. If this is you, reread Pointer 24. If the publication (with/by) pathway is causing too much anxiety, there is no harm about going back to a more traditional thesis. Perhaps it is time to rethink what you want out of your thesis.

With so many circumstances that can blow out your time schedules, worry can set in as thesis programs have time restrictions on completions. If you have serious fears that your thesis will not be completed on time, ask your supervisor(s) about an extension. There is usually wriggle room for extensions, but extensions take time. You may need to get help from your supervisor(s) to build an argument for an extension earlier than you think to show that your study has been adversely affected by circumstances, or that your study is more complex and demanding than initially expected. To complete on time, you might need to consider trimming the scope of your thesis to fit the time frame.

Scholarship holders may need to look at the terms and conditions of your scholarship to see if you can extend your candidature. You don't want funding from your home countries in the form of bursaries or grants to run out before you complete your thesis. Keep any agencies informed and get documentary evidence from supervisors to show that you have been working hard and will produce a great thesis, even if it is taking longer than intended.

If time is running out and you have been enrolled as a full-time student and money is an issue, you may want to change to part-time so that you can work on the side to keep money coming in. The earlier you ask for a change to part-time, the more time you will have to complete your thesis. Hopefully your new qualification will help balance the books down the track.

42. You are struggling to see yourself as a researcher

At some point in your thesis journey, you may question why you have embarked on your thesis journey. Feelings of inadequacy can be caused by many contributing factors such as the amount of time your thesis writing is taking, conflict with supervisors, or issues within your family and friends. Feelings of inadequacy can also be caused by your newly developing identity as a critical reader, an identity that writing your thesis has encouraged you to develop.

Even when things are going swimmingly well with your thesis, imposter syndrome can creep into your thesis journey. It is a very real and surprisingly common phenomenon in research. Even people who effectively manage highly responsible professional roles in industry can feel like it was a mistake to be let into a thesis program. Despite reassurances from supervisors and fellow students, you might feel like you are not capable of doing research. Imposter syndrome may resurface many times during the thesis journey, but the ironic thing is the more you put yourself out there and showcase your work, the more you will feel that your imposter syndrome is itself an imposter.

There are many ways of showcasing your work. These might include writing a blog, or perhaps writing a short general article for news outlets that promote recent research (with your supervisors or as a single-authored piece). Youtube videos about your experiences can be fun and you might get some interesting feedback. The Three Minute Thesis programs at universities (and sometimes in professional associations) are also a way of talking about your work in a different format. In these forums, it's important to listen to questions as these often give you insights into whether your audience has understood your work. If you are not sure what a question means, ask for the question to be repeated or explained. Getting some feedback from your supervisor(s) will help too.

You might like to push yourself in other ways, by giving a short seminar to fellow postgraduate students or preparing a short PowerPoint presentation for your supervisor(s) at your next supervision meeting. These are small steps that let you rehearse your academic voice so that you can feel more confident about yourself as a researcher. If you have collected your data and partly analyzed it, you might like to present at larger conferences where you can test out your ideas before writing them up in your thesis. If giving presentations at conferences sounds terrifying, you might think about a friendlier option such as a postgraduate conference or co-presenting with another graduate student, or even your supervisor(s). With each step you might feel a bit braver about your ideas.

There are still other ways to begin to rid yourself of imposter syndrome. Having realistic goals for writing helps maintain forward momentum. Consider the best times of day for productive writing and how much you really need to produce to meet your goals. Try writing small chunks and have a critical friend read over what you have written. If you can do this on a regular basis, you may feel less overwhelmed. Once you begin to feel more confident, try writing larger sections for sustained periods of time.

To get your writing to flow, you can think about how you like to get your writing started. Do you like to write a 'flow of consciousness' putting down on paper whatever thoughts come to mind? Do you like to make bullet points and then elaborate? Some thesis writers like a pomodoro technique where you break your time into 25-minute chunks with five-minute rests, so you are working with time, rather than against it (Cirillo, 2018). Try different approaches until you find something that does work for you. You may find your writing issue is less about writing and more about approach.

43. Feedback!

Getting the right type and amount of feedback from supervisors is a problem experienced by many thesis writers (Chugh, Macht & Harreveld, 2022). There can be either too much or too little feedback, and sometimes comments might not appear to be constructive. You may feel that you are being misunderstood or ignored. CAPITAL LETTERS or certain types of phrasing can make you feel like you are being screamed at!

While we all know that positive, constructive feedback helps you move forward with your writing, negative or inadequate feedback can fuel a fear of putting words on paper. Negative feedback has the potential to affect your emotional well-being and evoke any number of negative feelings.

But what constitutes negative feedback varies from person to person. Perhaps you are someone who wants your supervisor to explain what you are doing well, whereas your supervisor wants to focus on how you can improve what might already be good. When your text is full of comments, it can mean that you have caught your supervisor's attention and their comments are asking for more. 'Please explain, more details! Perhaps move these paragraphs around.' A text with few comments and the occasional positive note may mean that the supervisor doesn't know where to begin. If you feel a need to complain about feedback, it means that there is a mismatch between your expectations and the feedback being delivered.

If the quality and/or quantity of feedback is causing you distress, whether because you are not reading each other in the right way or because your supervisor is just grumpy, you need to remedy this early through dialogue. If you don't speak up about your feedback in supervision meetings, you won't get the guidance you need to make required changes. If you are afraid to speak up, you could possibly take a friend along to the next meeting (but let your supervisor(s) know this and your reasons for wanting to do so in advance).

If you don't understand what your supervisor(s') feedback is intended to achieve, one possibility is to ask for a summary paragraph to guide your reading of their feedback. Supervisors may be commenting on everything to be helpful, without thinking how to arrange their comments so you can identify your priority areas. If this is the case, it is certainly worth having a conversation with your supervisor(s) to discuss the kind/amount of feedback you are receiving, so you understand the important issues and can deal with them first.

Sometimes any feedback can feel like an attack on you. One interesting conundrum of thesis writing is the more of you that you put into your writing, the more the feedback on your thesis will seem personal. While a critique of your writing might make you scream 'they don't like me!', it is what has been written that is at issue. So rather than seeing feedback as a personal attack, think of it as giving insight into how to empower your researcher identity. You will certainly need to respond to feedback from your examiners in an analytical manner, so, in some ways, your supervisors' feedback is preparing you for this. It's good to look at critical feedback as a positive thing as it helps you move forward. You might consider feedback from supervisors as a step towards learning the art of critical self-reflection. If you don't get any feedback from your supervisor(s), this is far more problematic.

Learning how to take criticism of your writing can be challenging. You may find it useful to distance your emotional responses by taking an analysis of the specific comments that your supervisor(s) have raised. Drawing up a table with the individual comments on one side, and your responses on the other, might be a helpful strategy. As academics, we all need to understand how to respond to feedback when publishing in journals, where critical feedback is the expected norm. There is also nothing wrong with having a good cry if it helps. Understanding why some of your writing is not clearly understood is crucial to learning how to write like a researcher.

As you progress through your research and thesis writing, you will begin to feel more in control of the direction of your work and become more autonomous. Knowing this is normal might help you be patient with yourself and others. It will all come right in the long term. Feedback is like learning to dance on a flying carpet. It's exhilarating when you stop panicking about falling off!

44. It's not the right time for your thesis

There are life events that necessitate a change in direction, or you may have just come to a decision that research is not for you after all. Before giving up, think carefully about your reasons.

In life things rarely go to plan, and there can be major curveballs. Even though you thought that it was a good time to write that thesis, life events get in the way that can make it seem too hard. The pandemic of COVID-19 certainly presented all manner of unexpected obstacles and hurdles: children home all day; a partner working from home, losing their job; your flatmates at home all the time, and you can't find a quiet place to work. You (or your family) can get very sick or you or someone in your family might have experienced a physical or emotional trauma. If you are just starting your thesis and it's clear that things are not going to get better anytime soon, you might want to stop and recommence when things improve. There is no shame in this. Some universities will let you have an extension, or even take a leave of absence and return to your studies in a year or two. Your circumstances will determine how long you might need. Be sure to talk with your supervisor(s) about any concerns earlier rather than later. They are aware of the regulations and can support you.[3] You really shouldn't try to manage on your own. It takes time to heal, so be kind to yourself and take all the time you need. Universities have support that you can access.

In other instances, the reasons that you embarked on your thesis-writing project have dissipated. What would happen if, for example, you were offered a promotion or your dream job before you finished your thesis? Would you still have the same passion and drive to complete? Do you need to finish your thesis to develop the professional identity you envisaged? Your new professional role might be very demanding, especially when you start a new role. Your new role may have new responsibilities and commitments. Think about options. Will your new role allow for study leave in the foreseeable future? Will you have to relocate? If you were attending your university in person, could you reasonably change to an online format? If your new role is not related to your thesis topic, can you change your topic to get best value from your thesis? What are your options for deferring or changing to part-time study? If none of these options are available or excite you, perhaps it is best to think about moving on.

For some of you, you may have gone into thesis writing to satisfy family or friends and you are finding that it does not work for you. If your heart is not in your thesis and you are finding yourself struggling throughout your thesis journey to just keep going, the logical conclusion may be that the whole process of writing a thesis is just not your thing. Family may have high expectations, but in most cases their ultimate priority is for you to be happy. Deciding to do something else may be the best decision you can make. Putting a stop on your thesis is a decision that you need to be comfortable with now, and in the future. You need to talk through your decision with interested parties. These can range from community elders to work colleagues to family or friends. University counselling services can help you talk through what you want and need to say. You need to have honest conversations about how you are feeling.

Talk through your reasons for wanting to stop with your supervisors. They can help you with the administrative tasks involved. If a thesis is not for you, dealing with it sooner will avoid a lot of unnecessary stress later. If your decision is not to proceed through to the end, remember to take time to appreciate what you have learned about being a researcher and writer, and what you have learned about who you are and who you want to be. None of this will ever be wasted!

Notes

1 Common signs of distress are: Eating or sleeping too much or too little; Pulling away from people and things; Having low or no energy; Having unexplained aches and pains, such as constant stomachaches or headaches; Feeling helpless or hopeless; Excessive smoking, drinking, or using drugs, including prescription medications; Worrying a lot of the time and feeling guilty but not sure why; Thinking of hurting yourself or someone else; Having difficulty readjusting to home or work life. https://www.samhsa.gov/find-help/disaster-distress-helpline/warning-signs-risk-factors

2 Supervisors have prescribed workloads in most universities, and you need to check if they have the capacity to take on an additional candidate.

3 Universities have well-documented procedures for delay, either extension, deferral or changing from full-time to part-time. Read through the documentation carefully to help you work out your best approach.

References

Carter, Susan, Blumenstein, Marion, & Cook, Catherine. (2013). Different for women? The challenges of doctoral studies. *Teaching in Higher Education*, 18(4), 339–351. https://doi.org/10.1080/13562517.2012.719159

Chugh, Ritesh, Macht, Stephanie, & Harreveld, Bobby. (2022). Supervisory feedback to postgraduate research students: A literature review. *Assessment & Evaluation in Higher Education*, 47(5), 683–697. https://doi.org/10.1080/02602938.2021.1955241

Cirillo, Francesco. (2018). *The Pomodoro technique: The life-changing time-management system*. Random House.

González-Betancor, Sara M., & Dorta-González, Pablo. (2020). Risk of interruption of doctoral studies and mental health in PhD students. *Mathematics*, 8(10), 1695–1707. https://doi.org/10.3390/maths8101695

Hunter, Kay H., & Devine, Karen. (2016). Doctoral students' emotional exhaustion and intentions to leave academia. *International Journal of Doctoral Studies*, 11(2), 35–61. http://doi.org/10.289945/3396

Wisker, Gina, & Robinson, Gillian. (2013). Doctoral 'orphans': Nurturing and supporting the success of postgraduates who have lost their supervisors. *Higher Education Research & Development*, 32(2), 300–313. https://doi.org/10.1080/07294360.2012.657160

7 Finally done!

Overview

Chapter 7 assumes that you have weathered all the dramas life has thrown at you, and you have submitted your great work. It is a time to stop for a moment and fully appreciate your success.

The time between submitting your thesis for examination and receiving the examiners' reports is a rollercoaster ride of emotions. You have the exhilaration that comes with submitting your thesis and yet still live in terror of your examiners' judgements. You are feeling completely exhausted, or perhaps still in a panic that your thesis is not perfect. You are most probably relieved at reaching this end point. This is a time where you start to think about exploring your professional future, and transitioning from one academic identity into another. It can be a time for great academic productivity as you contemplate reshaping your thesis writing into other genres for wider readership.

This chapter aims to help you get through the postpartum void that often coincides with the submission of your thesis. In the pages that follow, we present you with our final pointers. These ask you to reflect on how you can reconnect with family and friends and rebuild relationships if you have let them slide. Then we ask you to consider a potential new set of academic identities, those of a new graduate and an emerging researcher, and what this might mean for you professionally once your thesis is complete. We advise you about possible ways to change your thesis into a book and explore some of the ways that your research work and your freshly minted academic identities could be exploited by scammers. In our final pointer, we give words of advice for addressing your examination reports, if your thesis program allows for editing.

DOI: 10.4324/9781003323402-7

Figure 7.1   You've submitted. What comes next?

45. Take a moment to celebrate your achievement

At the beginning of this book, we explained how writing a thesis shared similarities to the ways that a potter creates a pot. In that story we reflected on how a potter needs to centre themselves in their work. When this happens, through every stage of production, the initial throwing, the turning, decorating and finishing, each piece of pottery becomes unique with its own beauty and strengths. Each small feature shows off the power and thought of its maker. Your thesis is no different.

You have researched and written your thesis. You have had feedback and rewritten large parts of your thesis many times. Every decision that you made has helped to create your final work to submit for examination.

This is a significant milestone in your life – one that you have put in so much time and effort to reach. Take time to relax. After you have submitted, there is nothing you can change until you get the reports back from your examiners. Avoid the temptation to look at your thesis. You will torture your-self if you reread your thesis and find a typo or two. Let the examiners do their job. You submitted; you have passed a milestone!

It's time for a little celebration for you and all those who have travelled this journey with you. Now is the time to thank yourself and those who sup-ported you, your family, friends, supervisors and anyone else in your aca-demic community that has helped you in your thesis journey. Take a break now and cross something off that bucket list that has been steadily growing while you have been stuck in front of a computer screen. Don't wait until after your examiners' reports come back, as examiners will always ask for some more work.

You can celebrate and thank your supporters again when you pass!

46. So what happens now? The postpartum void

After gestating this small nugget of new knowledge – learning new practices, developing new research skills – you have finally delivered. Following the euphoria of submitting and celebrating, you may feel a void. You may have longed for time while you have been writing to deadlines, but now you may feel you have excessive time on your hands while you await your examiners reports.

While you dedicated your time to research and endless writing, others stepped in to fill the space you left and took some of your responsibilities. You can't simply pick up where you left off. While some friends, family and work colleagues will be glad to have you step back in and return to old ways, not everything can return to pre-thesis conditions. If you have been juggling employment with your thesis writing, it might be difficult for others to hand you back those extra responsibilities. The same may apply to your family responsibilities. Some of your original jobs are now occupied by oth-ers. New routines have been created. Stepping back into your previous role can disturb and disrupt those routines. The longer you spent working on your thesis, the more changes have taken place. Take time to appreciate what family members have done for you and think about whether you want to start afresh. You may still want your children to iron their own shirts, and they might even be offended if you suddenly start to do this for them.

Pre-thesis friends have also moved on in their lives and you might be left wondering where they have all gone. They might have discovered new trendy coffee places, or places to eat, and not kept you entirely in the loop. Your friends from your academic community might still be working on their thesis and not have time to linger over lunch. Now would be an excellent time to make a meal for those friends, do a bit of child-minding to help them get ahead on their theses. Readjusting your social activities will take time. Use some of your free time to help those who have helped you.

Take some of your free time to reinvigorate and reflect. The void will fill quickly enough as you reposition yourself in the light of your new identity of 'thesis completer'!

47. Welcome to the next step on your professional journey

Now that you have submitted your thesis, it's time to review your professional identity. Do your previous professional identities, with the roles and responsibilities attached, still feel like a good fit for you? For some of you, slipping back into your previous or existing role will feel good. For others, you may be looking for new professional opportunities. Thesis writing, and the research that lies behind it, will have equipped you with a whole range of new skills and approaches, and new professional networks. You may have different world views that have arisen from your thesis topic, your thesis methodology and even from your thesis field of study. You now have more in your work skills repertoire than you had before, and this could mean that your previous or existing job is no longer as satisfying.

Now might be the time to ask for that promotion or to ask your employer for new responsibilities. Or there might be greener fields elsewhere. You may need to go hunting for a more interesting and appropriate job.[1] This is an opportune time to think about how your new skills can help you to move to something or somewhere different.

Some of you will turn your attention to writing.

48. A heads up for writing in a different genre

Now that you have finished your thesis, many of you will want to publish all or parts of it. Some of you might want to convert your thesis into a book or rewrite some of the content of your thesis as a book chapter or journal article. Perhaps you have already begun this journey. For those of you who are just beginning to think about publication, here are a couple of tips that you might want to consider.

You may think that a book is the easiest option. Unfortunately, many publishers have a policy of not accepting theses. If you have no publication history (journal articles etc.) to your name, your chances of publishing your thesis as a book are even less likely. For those of you who want to accept the challenge, you need to think about a book as a different genre from a thesis (see Biber & Conrad [2019] for an overview of different types of genres) and look at how you can reshape it for a different audience. Your audience is no longer your examiners, the main purpose of your writing has changed.

To redesign your thesis into a book, you can start with a few relatively easy changes. Even though these are easy tasks, they can be daunting. You need to be prepared to change your text. During the thesis journey, you have learned how to edit. This is your golden opportunity to use those editing skills.

Because your introductory chapter has a new audience, it has a new focus. The chapter now needs to be centred on why this book was written, what it aims to contribute (and how), and who might be interested in reading it. The introductory chapter to your book no longer aims to show a gap in a field; it is now a sales pitch, one that can make or break your book proposal.

The next part to tackle is your literature review. Some books written by some academic publishers contain a slimmed-down chapter labelled 'important work in the field' but many do not. Your literature review in your book is typically embedded in your sales pitch as a page or two in your introductory chapter. Your literature review serves as evidence for your argument about why your book was written and what it aims to contribute.[2]

Your methodology chapter requires some general editing as well. In a book, there is usually no need to demonstrate your knowledge of different types of research designs, no need to discuss your pilot study, or even the reasons for your coding. While the methodology chapter in your thesis is often quite lengthy, it may be only a few pages in your introductory chapter.

By now you are probably wondering what else is left. Your findings! This is the guts of your book. This is typically what a book is all about. While your findings receive greater emphasis in a book than in your thesis, they still may need to be more streamlined. There is no requirement to include extensive background details in your book. If your thesis has separate sections for the findings and discussion, you might consider combining your data and analysis together (see Pointer 21). If you have more than one research question (or your research question has more than one part), you might want to explore each in a separate chapter. You may even want to delete a research question or create a slightly different one. You can think about additional ways to structure what you want to say. Your book and your thesis are different things. Don't be afraid to think about different ways of presenting your content. If your data is derived from interviews, you might organize these into individual stories, where different people introduce different experiences. When thinking about restructuring possibilities, think of the different ways that you can capture readers' attention or tell an interesting story that makes an important point in a way that will appeal to a wide audience.

The concluding chapter of your thesis could do with a bit of editing as well. The conclusion of a book doesn't need to demonstrate knowledge. There is no need for extensive repetition in the concluding chapter. Your concluding chapter is often only a few pages, summarizing the aims of the book and how your book has made its own unique contribution.

As you may have gathered, a book reaches out to its audience. Given the tone of many theses can be rather impersonal, you may want to introduce more personalized ways of being and doing that we have introduced throughout this book.

If you are interested in writing your book, the place to start is with the book proposal. Some publishers accept a sample chapter or two with your book proposal, while others want the entire manuscript. When you put in your proposal to the publisher, note that while the content of the book is derived from a thesis, it has been/will be completely rewritten. Expect that your book to take a minimum of a year of hard work to complete and expect to wait up to six months before you get a response on the outcome. If you are lucky, you will complete the task faster than expected and the publisher will take a shorter time to respond.

Publishing a book doesn't exclude you from publishing part of your thesis as a journal article. While publishers don't like too much of your thesis to have been published, they like to see that you are ready for the publication game. In some cases, you may be able to use the content of a previously published journal article as part of your book (with permissions). If you are submitting a proposal that asks for a sample chapter or two, you might want to submit your existing publication as one of them.

Publishing a journal article on the same content as your thesis has some additional advantages. It is a useful way of promoting your book. Once you have your book proposal accepted, you can self-cite the upcoming book in your article as a way of getting it noticed.

Whatever you decide to do, remember to enjoy the experience, as every experience increases your skills and helps you move towards future success.

For further insights and ideas, read Laura Belcher's (2009) book on academic publishing; Rowena Murray's (2013) work on writing for academic journals; and Laura Portwood-Stacer's (2021) volume on writing scholarly book proposals.

49. Traps for the unwary

Scam artists abound in all aspects of life, so don't be surprised to find these predators lurking around in your academic world.

Globally, reputable publishers have long developed the system of peer review and this system of blind reviews acts to ensure that the research material published is verified by leaders in the field. The system is not foolproof and there are plenty of ways scammers have found to monetize your research.

Thesis scammers disguised as thesis publishers make you offers that you dreamed about as you slaved over your thesis. There, in your inbox, is the offer to publish your thesis in full! These are usually pay-to-publish predators. The book publisher is unknown with no credibility so there is little or no value in publishing with them. If there is a statement with a request for money, stay clear.

There are also predatory journals that offer to publish your work quickly, at a cost. They do not conduct peer-review procedures and expect you to pay for the privilege of being in print. Some even have fake impact factors, rankings and sometimes even an editorial board that uses legitimate academics' names but without their knowledge.

Predatory conferences are relatively new in the academic landscape. These conferences either don't exist (fake conferences) or they are set up to make a fulsome profit for the organizers. Make sure you carefully check out all conferences, especially those asking you to present your work. There are lots of credible conferences from which you can choose.

There will also be offers in your inbox to redesign/reconfigure your work for different audiences. For example, you may receive offers to have your book chapter turned into a feature article or to make your book into a video clip. While some of these offers could be legitimate and might be exactly what you need, read the fine print carefully and discuss the offer with your supervisor(s) or other experienced academics before you commit. Ask your supervisor(s) for other potential publication outlets and look where other researchers in your area publish. Journals that have published an article in one area might like another companion piece, if you can show that it makes a substantial contribution to the area.

If you are interested in learning more about the perils in publishing your research, you might like to read 'Combatting predatory academic journals and conferences', a report prepared by the Interacademy Partnership in 2022.

50. Getting your examination results

The moment you have been eagerly awaiting and dreading has arrived, and you have finally got your examination reports. While statistics are in your favor (the vast majority of thesis writers pass [Mewburn, 2020]), examination reports can be terrifying, frustrating and overwhelming. This is where you need to create a 'distanced' identity. If you have passed (as most thesis writers do), the comments are meant to help you. But it is easy to get disheartened. You've worked so hard on your thesis. You might do well to look at the comments as if they were written for someone else or ask a friend to read you the positive comments, perhaps multiple times. There are good things in your writing. There has to be. You have passed!

If you have written an undergraduate thesis where you can't make any corrections, think about the positives in your thesis and bring those out when you want to present your work at a conference, or when you want to write up parts of the thesis as a journal article or book chapter. If you have written a master's by research or a doctorate, you will likely need to attend to the feedback. Most thesis writers get anxious when they see a written critique of their work. If feedback upsets you, wait a little while before you attempt to address the comments. You need a clear head. Almost everyone has some revisions to make on their thesis.[3]

For a very small minority, revisions will involve fixing the odd typo, a dodgy reference, and formatting. Most thesis writers need to do a little more. This might include explaining a paragraph or section more clearly or refining one of your key terms. Sometimes changes can sound enormous, when in fact all that is really needed is a few sentences or a paragraph in the right place to clarify a point. Perhaps your examiners ask for you to move a section to another location, or to add another small section or two. These changes can usually be done within four weeks. What's an extra month of your life in the larger scheme of things? Sometimes, examiners can ask for a major change. This usually involves asking for more of something: a more extensive literature review, a more detailed methodology, a deeper analysis of the data. In a few instances, there may be methodological inconsistencies that you need to address. These are all manageable.

As a researcher and thesis writer, you have learned valuable skills in resilience and patience. Bite your last remaining bullet and get on with it. You don't want to throw away years of your life and a future career just because you have a little more work to do. Most of you will probably think the revisions are more drastic than they were intended to be. Don't procrastinate. The size of the corrections will likely grow inside your head while you delay. Universities often puts time deadlines on the revision process. The longer you procrastinate, the less time you have. The sooner you complete the corrections, the sooner you graduate.

Before you start your revisions, ask your supervisor(s) for guidance about how to approach the changes. You are not likely the first thesis writer they have supervised. They have valuable insights about how to manage changes.

After you have a plan in place you can start work on making the requested or required changes. Keep track of any changes you make in your thesis so that you can demonstrate how you have responded to your examiners' reports. In some cases, you will only need your main supervisor or panel chair to sign off on the changes you make before the results can be confirmed through your university's administrative procedures.[4]

When your corrections have been made, the university will confirm your results and you can look forward to graduating! Now it is seriously time to celebrate, and to thank all those people who supported you one way or another through the journey.

Whether your thesis was for honors, a masters or a doctorate, it has been a very substantial undertaking. You have clung onto the thesis flying carpet and maybe even danced a little bit before you landed. There might have been a slip or two along the way, but you have learned how to create opportunities by confronting challenges. You are a more resilient person, more self-aware and ready for the next chapter in your life.

Well done, You!

Notes

1 Career advice services offered by the university can provide useful perspectives on your opportunities. Networks developed during thesis writing can be productive avenues to new employment.
2 Check if there is an existing review of your literature on your chosen topic in the public domain. If not, you could think about your literature review chapter as a starting for that review paper.
3 A useful strategy is to create a simple table with the recommended actions on one side, and the actions you undertake (or plan to undertake) on the other side.
4 In a very small number of cases, a thesis will be protected from publication (embargoed). This is to protect the author from harm should the research present knowledge that may be seen as potentially hostile to powerful forces.

References

Belcher, Laura. (2009). *Writing your journal article in 12 weeks: A guide to academic publishing success*. Sage.

Biber, Douglas, & Conrad, Susan. (2019). *Register, genre, style*. (2nd ed.). Cambridge University Press.

InterAcademy Partnership. (2022). Combatting predatory academic journals and conferences. https://apo.org.au/sites/default/files/resource-files/2022-03/apo-nid316970.pdf

Mewburn, Inger. (2020). *How to tame your PhD*. Thesiswhisperer Books. https://thesiswhisperer.com

Murray, Rowena. (2013). *Writing for academic journals*. (3rd ed.). Open University Press.

Portwood-Stacer, Laura. (2021). *The book proposal book: A guide for scholarly authors*. Princeton University Press.

Shmatko, Natalia, et al. (2020). The value of PhD in the changing world of work: Traditional and alternative research careers. *Technological Forecasting & Social Change*, 152, 119907. https://doi.org/10.1016/j.techfore.2019.119907

Index

Pages followed by "n" refer to notes.

For Product Safety Concerns and Information please contact our EU
representative GPSR@taylorandfrancis.com
Taylor & Francis Verlag GmbH, Kaufingerstraße 24, 80331 München, Germany

www.ingramcontent.com/pod-product-compliance
Ingram Content Group UK Ltd.
Pitfield, Milton Keynes, MK11 3LW, UK
UKHW021456080625
459435UK00012B/523